The *New*
Cross-Country
Ski Book

John Caldwell

The Stephen Greene Press *Brattleboro, Vermont*

Grateful acknowledgment is made to the following photographers for their pictures used in this book:

Robert F. George for the title-page photo and Nos. 1, 2, 9, 10, 11, 12, 13, 14, 17, 18, 21, 22, 23, 24, 25, 26, 27, 28, 29, 30, 31, 33, 34, 36, 37, 38, 39, 40, 41, 42, 44 and 47.

Richard L. Harris for Nos. 5, 6, 7, 15, 16, 32, 43, 45 and 52.

The Canadian Pacific Railway for No. 3; Larry McDonald for 4; T. J. Caldwell for 8 and 46; Bob Davis for 19; Nancy Simmerman for 20; J. H. Caldwell for 35; American-Swedish News Exchange, New York City, for 48; Asa Ramsay for 49; Peter Marcus for 50, and William L. Smith for 51.

Third Edition, 1971

This book has been produced in the United States of America: designed by R. L. Dothard Associates, printed and bound by Springfield Printing Corp.

It is published by The Stephen Greene Press, Brattleboro, Vt. 05301.

Library of Congress Catalog Card Number: 71-173400
International Standard Book Number: 0-8289-0137-6

Contents

1. *"Thanks, Mom—that's great."*

How far we've come

When I wrote the first book on cross-country ("x-c") skiing in 1964 the sport was little appreciated in North America. So, because only a relatively small number of hardy souls knew what it was all about in those days, I dug deep and told how to cut down wooden (*wooden,* mind you) downhill skis, explained the differences between Alpine and x-c gear— and in general took an elementary approach to the whole subject.

How times change! For instance, during the 1940's and '50's most of the recognized x-c skiing was done by racers. We have had Olympic Teams in the Nordic events since the '30's, for that matter, and it's been teams like these, as well as college and school teams, which have provided the focus on the sport.

New interest, new approach

Beginning in the '60's, though, many snowbelt families really began showing an interest in x-c. But even during the early part of the decade there was only one annual open x-c tour race, and it drew less than 100 skiers; in 1971, just three of the established open races totaled more than 1,000 finishers. Furthermore, at this writing the United States has over twenty well-entrenched firms importing x-c equipment, compared to a handful ten years ago. And skiers nowadays are examining the virtues of some ten brands of Hard Blue wax instead of wondering what "blue wax" is.

Today, therefore, I feel that a differently weighted approach is called for, and this has been my plan in rewriting the book.

Learning from the best

Much of the more detailed information hereafter has been prompted by queries I've received from the general public since the first edition was published. Part of it, though—specifically, on technique, training and waxing—describes new methods I've worked out with the welcome help of America's top skiers.

I believe that almost anyone can ski cross-country, and that the vast majority of skiers welcomes at least being able to read about the best techniques, equipment, waxes, and so on. I know that if I was taking a lesson in golf and the instructor started me out with a "beginner's swing," whatever that might be, I'd bop him over the head with my club. I want to know how Nicklaus hits the ball. Even if I can't do it that way, I want to be able to try. I refuse to get shook up when I hit my ball into the rough or miss the darned thing completely. I'm out for enjoyment and shoot around 100.

It's important to recognize that the racing crowd generally sets the styles. They also tend to get the most publicity. It's similar to the auto-racing group. The miles driven by the racers do not begin to approach those driven by the rest of the motorists, but the race-car people are the ones who, to a large extent, test new equipment, come up with ideas for engines and other automotive innovations.

The x-c racers do the same. They have been most generous in sharing their knowledge with the public during the past few years, and this attitude is a tribute to themselves and to their interest in the sport.

Thus I'll refer sometimes to racers, or racing situations, partly to clarify a point, partly for color, and partly out of respect for the racers who have done so much for ski touring. But nowadays you can be sure that most of the x-c'ers in North America are tourskiers and it's for them primarily that this book is written.

The hardest job has been condensing. I would like to write 300 pages each on waxing, technique, equipment or training, but they would be extremely technical—and probably a drag to the average family skier. So while this book contains lots of information, please don't think it is offered as the last word for the aspiring Olympic skier.

It's your own thing

All of which brings me to my over-all feeling about x-c. It's my main pitch and hasn't changed.

2. First rule for x-c: have fun your way.

Cross-country skiing should be fun for everyone. The range of possibilities for enjoyment is unlimited. You can ski anywhere there's snow, you can use a wide variety of equipment, you can ski alone or with a group, you can use the very best technique while wearing the clothes you just picked up from the local rummage sale, or you can wear the latest styles and invent your own technique. So pick out and use anything you want from this book—but most of all, *have fun skiing x-c.* Make it be *your* thing.

No word games

Just two more points.

First, I use "cross-country skiing," "ski touring" and "running" interchangeably throughout. Some people insist that the phrase "cross-country skiing" means something very rugged, or something nearly approaching racing. To me, cross-country skiing means skiing across the countryside. A simple, literal translation. In the comparatively few places where I think it more helpful to differentiate between x-c casual skiing and x-c racing I will just flag the sections which refer to racing.

Next, this is not a book on ski-mountaineering. The business of overnight trips, coping in avalanche country, special equipment including skins, packs and cooking utensils are things I am not going to treat. They have all been well covered in the several mountaineering publications.

Cross-country scrapbook

Everyone's memories of a favorite sport are different, but all, really, are vignettes of people. Like Canada's Herman "Jackrabbit" Johannsen, a spry 65, below (3)—and now, in his mid-90's, ready for the 1971-72 season, and skiing six hours a day. And like John Bower, right (4), shortly before winning in 1968 one of x-c's most coveted trophies: the King's Cup for the Holmenkollen Combined, in Norway. His achievement is the greatest to date for any U.S. Nordic skier.

5 & 6. There are veteran tourskiers like Archer Winsten of the N.Y. *Post* (above) and Rudi Mattesich of The Ski Touring Council.

And it's international competitors like the U.S. Team's "big three" (8, above)—from left to right: Mike Gallagher, Bob Gray and Mike Elliott —at spring training camp in Colorado in 1971, and, at right, Martha Rockwell, America's No. 1 woman x-c skier (9).

And it's kids like these (7, left), getting waxing tips from Dr. Eric Barradale, who sparked U.S. interest in tour races with his Washington's Birthday open event. First run in 1963, this prototype race draws over 500 skiers, including Olympic runners and first-graders.

Equipment

The supply of x-c equipment has increased fast enough to keep up with the growing number of converts. Several years ago it was a rare sporting goods store that carried x-c gear, but now it's nearly a buyer's paradise. The European manufacturers are jostling to corner the U.S. market, and meanwhile firms in this country are already producing boots, poles and clothing. So if you take the time to look around you should be able to find anything from real racing gloves to good, rugged touring skis.

Since there is so much to choose from, a few basic points are well to keep in mind:

1. If your dealer really knows x-c and can service you well, his expertise can be more important to you than whether he carries a special make or not. There are many good brands of equipment, so don't get hung up on just one in particular.

2. If you have a chance to talk with someone knowledgeable about x-c—or better yet, if you have a chance to use some equipment before making a purchase—you will be able to make a better choice. For instance, one of the first things to do is try different widths in skis (see why, below). You could also try different weights in boots and different lengths in poles.

3. You can spend anywhere from $60.00 to over $100.00 for a complete set of equipment: skis, boots, bindings, poles and wax. The more expensive equipment may not be the best suited for your needs. As I will explain, you may prefer an all-wood ski, which is usually less expensive than other skis containing at least some synthetic materials.

The skis

If you want to be exact and measure x-c skis for width at their tips as well as right under the binding point, you will come up with perhaps a hundred different combinations of widths. For purposes of simplification I group skis in three different categories, according to width under the binding: touring skis are about 55–60 millimeters (2¼ inches) wide under the foot; light touring skis, about 52–56 mm (2 inches); racing skis, 48–50 mm (under 2 inches). Each ski has special advantages.

The touring ski

Tourers are slightly wider than most x-c skis and therefore are heavier, stiffer, more rugged and less wobbly. They usually weigh between 5 and 6 pounds. Many beginners prefer these skis because they provide more stability and are easy to learn the sport on. Some of the deep-powder addicts in the western parts of North America use the wider skis, which of course don't sink as deep in the snow as the narrower versions do.

The light touring ski

The light touring ski is enough narrower, lighter and more flexible to feel like a racing ski in comparison with the touring ski described above. But don't be scared off: this is the ski I would recommend for most skiers, even beginners. Lots of people I know have started with the wide tourers, only to go to narrower skis very quickly after discovering how easy x-c skiing is.

Anyway, the trend is definitely toward lighter equipment. Tracks and trails are better every year, and can accommodate the narrower skis. Skiers' abilities, too, are improving; and in a sport where much emphasis is on freedom of movement and lightness of equipment, these are the skis that make the most sense for the most people.

I even know a few tourskiers who have racing skis on hand as spares, or just in case they happen to want to enter a little race some day.

The racing ski

The racing ski is super light, narrow and fragile. Mine weigh less than 3½ pounds. These skis are designed specifically for racing, or skiing fast, on well-prepared tracks, and if you try them out in the boondocks and snap off a tip you have no one to blame but yourself. These skis rarely hold up for a season with an inexperienced skier. In fact, some top racers use their skis up during the winter, one way or another.

Coaches make a mistake when they start their neophytes on racing skis. A couple of bad skiing days with poor tracks, combined with some rough skiers, and the athletic department ends up with a bunch of kindling wood.

Use these skis carefully.

Summarizing: The wider the ski the more it weighs, the more rugged it is and less likely to break. The narrowest, lightest skis are the fastest and most maneuverable, and the most fragile. The light touring ski is a very good compromise in flexibility and ruggedness. If you begin with this one you will probably stick to it unless you get serious about running and switch to racing skis.

Ski construction

Most of the skis being produced at this writing are still made of wood, with the better models containing several laminations. These laminations, which make the skis stronger and reduce chances of warping, give the manufacturers something to play around with. Many different woods can be used, varying the strength, weight and flexibility of the skis. Some makers even leave out a few laminations in the center of the ski in an effort to decrease the weight; such air channels are found primarily in the racing types, and, no matter what anyone says, they do not add to the strength of the ski.

There are also some fiberglass skis on the market. Some are laminated, some not. But in either case, they are all very rugged and won't give you many breakage problems.

A number of companies in the United States and Scandinavia are experimenting with synthetic materials in x-c skis. Perhaps the pattern the Alpine industry followed in going from wood to almost all metal/ fiberglass construction will take place here in the Nordic world. Right now, though, traditionalists are sticking with the wood skis for a couple of reasons at least: The right flexibility, or feel, has not been perfectly reproduced as yet in the synthetic skis; and the wax still holds better on wood bottoms.

Flexibility

If you're paying only $25.00 to $35.00 for a pair of skis it may be too much to expect to get skis with a good flex. But if you look around, and have a choice, you may be able to help your skiing pleasure by choosing skis with the proper flex. This flexibility and camber are related, but not so completely that the ski can be judged by camber alone. So here are three little tests that will help:

1. You can give skis the squeeze test. Hold them, bottoms facing, and squeeze—simple! They should come together evenly the entire length. The tips will separate a little. Now grab another pair of skis and squeeze them. If you test enough skis you will notice that some are softer than others.

In general, if you have a ski the right length, you need a slightly more soft (i.e., flexible) ski if you are light for your height, and a slightly stiffer ski if you are, shall I say, rugged for your height.

2. Here's a very interesting one. Put the skis on a smooth, hard floor; stand on them and try slipping a piece of paper under them where your feet are. If the paper slides between the floor and the skis comfortably, these skis are right for you. If the paper doesn't slide under, the skis are too soft. If there is a big gap and you could slide several pieces of paper underneath (or a piece of cardboard), the skis are too stiff.

3. Finally, you can check the bottoms of your skis after a tour. If the wax is worn evenly, the skis are the right flex for you. If the wax is worn off on the tips and tails, the skis are too stiff. If the wax is worn off under the foot, the skis are too soft, or limber.

Of the extremes, it's better to have the skis a bit limber. At least this way you can use the wax under the foot—where it's very important—until it wears off. And a softer ski tends to track better.

Don't get too bothered by your skis' flex at first, because, if you're buying an inexpensive pair, finding the right degree of softness may be a matter of luck. It's also good to remember that, in general, stiff skis act better on hard or icy conditions, and soft skis better in powder. Most top runners have soft and stiff pairs of skis and use them according to conditions. So if your skis are a bit too soft or too stiff, chances are good that you will find they work O.K. all the time and especially well under certain conditions.

10. *Four x-c skis, of different widths and with different bottoms. Left to right: Hickory with lignostone edges, on a light touring ski; Neswood, on a light touring ski; hickory, on a race/training ski; and hickory with plastic edges, on a racing ski.*

The bottoms

The bottoms of your skis are important—after all, they're what you actually ski on. Of the different choices here I will make three categories: wood, nonwood, and those in between. (Photo 10)

> *Note:* Generally, the harder the ski bottom is the less well it holds wax; but even though the softer bottoms hold wax better, they wear out faster. So you should consider both these factors—tough bottoms and wax-holding ability—in making a choice.

Wood

The most popular wood bottom is hickory with lignostone edges. Because lignostone is compressed beechwood and very tough, it's used on the edges where most of the wear occurs; hickory is also a very tough wood. These bottoms are usually worth the extra expense for the tourskier.

Some skis have plastic edges instead of lignostone. These are good and tough too. They are also quite attractive.

In ruggedness, the next best wood bottom is an all-hickory one. These hold well against wear and tear.

Next in line is a softer wood bottom, usually birch, with hickory edges. Birch is lighter and not as tough as hickory but holds wax better. Most racing skis have this construction.

Don't look too hard for birch bottoms with lignostone or plastic edges. The manufacturers don't like this combination because the edges do not bond well with the birch. We once had some made in Norway for the U.S. Team, but practically had to hit the producer over the head to get them. We wanted the light birchwood on the bottom and then the tough edges. Since the edges are about 15 to 25 percent of the running surface of the ski, we reasoned it was important for a racer to have a fast edge: if the wax wore off the edges first, at least we'd have good edges left. Lignostone and plastic are both faster than bare wood. (By the way, the skis worked just fine.)

Finally, the less expensive skis have a one-piece bottom, usually birch. The construction is simpler, the wood is cheaper and softer. Obviously the edges wear quite fast, so it's a good idea to avoid these skis if you want something long-lasting.

In-between materials

Some skis have a wood bottom painted or treated with a plastic resin. These are proving out very well. The bottoms are rugged, fast, and they hold wax.

Another bottom is wood that has been impregnated with plastic prior to the lamination process. This N-wood, or neswood, is used by some furniture factories, especially in Finland. These ski bottoms are also tough, fast, and hold wax.

Either one of these bottoms, therefore, has advantages over wood: no pine-tar treatment of the ski is necessary, the bottom is hard and wears well, and it slides without wax under all conditions.

A third type in the in-between category is one painted with a thin layer of fiberglass. On some skis it's barely recognizable. For a few years these skis worked best under klister conditions, but now the fiberglass application has been improved so that it holds hard wax as well (beginners in x-c will find these terms explained in the Waxing chapter). The bottoms still scratch easily and are best left to the racing crowd.

Nonwood

Many manufacturers are trying for the molded fiberglass x-c ski. Pour material into a mold, set it—and bingo, out comes a ski. As I mentioned earlier, the flexibility problems have not yet been solved but I think you can expect an increasing number of these skis. They are *tough!* On many brands you can stand on the ski with one foot, and flatten the tip with the other foot. The tip bounces back and you're in business. These full fiberglass bottoms don't hold the wax quite as well as the wood bottoms, but with care you can do a good job with your waxing.

Another innovation is the so-called "fish scale" bottom. This has overlapping plastic scales (in appearance rather like a fish's) that are laid on like shingles from near the tip to the tail. The claim is that you never need wax. I've tried the skis and they work in klister conditions, or granular snow. I haven't had a chance to use them in powder yet. The skis actually sing as you ski. With each stride, or in going downhill, there is a slight hissing noise. This is something I'm not used to.

In summary: If you want to go the traditional route with preparing your ski bottoms—waxing and the whole bit—the wooden bottoms are the best. I think they'll be around for a long time. They do hold the wax best, and wax makes a difference, no matter how you slice it.

A good compromise is a plastic-impregnated or plastic-treated bottom. This eliminates the pine tar and is also very tough. You can hit a few sticks and stones, or ski on some ice, and not worry too much.

Finally, if waxing throws you off, by all means get a no-wax bottom. It's rugged and you never have to worry about snow conditions.

So far, our leading x-c skiers feel that most synthetic bottoms have sacrificed refinements in performance to save work in waxing, etc., and therefore the skis are not first-rate performers.

Ski lengths

The old standard still holds: *To measure your proper ski length, stand on the floor and reach up with your hand. Your ski should come to your wrist.*

If you are light for your height, you might find a slightly shorter ski more suitable. For instance, if you measure for a 205-centimeter ski (almost all skis are measured in cm's and you might as well get used to it—1 inch is about 2½ cm), you could get along on a 200-cm ski. If you are a bit on the heavy side for your height, a longer ski might be more suitable. As a rule, longer skis have a bit more stiffness to them.

Some people can reach about 225 cm, but they don't make many skis that long. I've seen 220-cm x-c skis, so they can be had. Most big people fare O.K. on 215's.

Other characteristics

The competition for the x-c ski market is producing many different looks for ski tops. You can get painted tops, plastic-coated tops, and natural tops. Next to a plastic top, skis treated with a good vinyl paint seem to wear the best, if you're interested in cosmetics.

One item to look for in a laminated ski is a tail protector built right into the ski. These help prevent the ski from splitting.

Some skis also have tip protectors, but I haven't found these necessary. If you have them, fine. If not, don't worry.

The bindings

The guys that were working hard to build better mousetraps must have shifted their focus to x-c bindings. I couldn't begin to describe all the different bindings that have come on the market recently. So I'll just classify them in two groups. I'll refer to *toe bindings*—ones that hold the boot on the ski by means of a device at the toe of the boot—and *heel cable bindings*—the ones that have heel cables as well as toepieces of some sort.

Toe bindings
Toe bindings include at least three categories:

1. The pin-binding has pins that stick up into the sole of the boot and a clamp (front throw) which exerts pressure downward on the sole of the boot at the toe. These bindings are simple, light, and inexpensive. We know they work; they've been used for years. Don't be afraid to stick with them in the face of pressure to use other types.

2. Another toe binding is one which holds the boot by some other means than the pins just described. Some hook into the top of the sole at the toe, others have pins which stick through the sole of the

11. *Close-up showing x-c racing boots and toe bindings. Note the freedom of the heel (and the heel plate under the left foot.)*

boot at the toe, and so on. Most of them are good; but, as I have said, I cannot describe all the variations here.

3. Finally, there are some step-in bindings on the market. One combination which is becoming popular has a metal piece on the toe of the boot that interlocks with the binding on the ski as you step in. This is very convenient, but has one major drawback: the boots and bindings are not interchangeable with other, different models.

Some other step-in bindings can be hitched or unhitched by use of the ski-pole point. Perhaps you've seen some advertised showing the pole pressing down on a front-throw release. These are fine too, but I always figured that when I was skiing I was after some exercise, for one thing, and so I don't mind bending over to fasten or unfasten my bindings. (I'm also one who actually bends over to pick up tennis balls; never could master that little bounce and pick-up with the racket, or the racket-heel lift.)

Heel cable bindings

Proponents of the cable binding argue that it offers some lateral support that is absent in the toe binding. This may be true, but I feel that lateral support is primarily a function of boot construction. (Many boots with a heel groove happen to be more rugged everywhere. If you want to make tests yourself, use a boot with a heel groove in it, first with a cable binding and then with a toe binding. I don't think you'll find much difference.)

Cable bindings are heavier than toe bindings but they do offer one advantage. If you have side hitches on your skis and can loop the cable through these, you will get more downpull on your boots and therefore will be able to ski downhill more in an Alpine manner—that is, with more edging and better control of your skis. Most ski-mountaineering people use a binding of this type. When they go uphill they unhitch the cable and can lift the heel freely.

> *Note:* It may be obvious, but I should tell you to be sure that the boot fits the binding. It's still possible to get poor fit, either because the binding is too wide for the boot sole, or because the boot sole is not the same shape as the binding sides. However, the manufacturers of most conventional bindings have got together with most of the boot manufacturers and now sizes and shapes are more standardized than before.
>
> One other caution. Be sure to get a boot that is compatible with your binding. Don't get a special step-in binding that requires a boot with a toepiece, without getting *that* boot, or *that* toepiece. Or, don't get a wide boot and a narrow binding.

Heel plates and pop-ups

You should have either a heel plate or a "pop-up." There are different sizes and shapes here too. Most of these are made of rubber or metal, or a combination of both, and are tacked on the ski right under the heel. They keep snow from balling up under your foot and offer some stability by virtue of the friction between them and the heel of the boot: the boot is less likely to slide off to the side of the ski.

Some skiers put a little piece of rubber, linoleum, or similar material

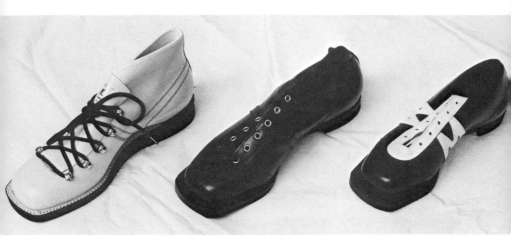

12. From left: touring boot, light touring boot and racing boot.

on the ski right next to the binding, under the ball of the foot. This helps to keep the snow from piling up between the boot and binding.

The boots

You should suit your boots to your skis, which in turn should be suited to your bent and your terrain. Therefore the range of boots is similar to that of skis. There are rugged models which are usually heavier and stiffer than most touring boots; these would match up with the touring skis. Then there are light touring boots and racing boots. From the touring boots you can go all the way down in lightness and flexibility to the racing boot that weighs as little as 24 ounces. (Photos 12 and 13)

Touring boots

These boots, which closely approximate downhill boots in size and shape, are well designed for rugged touring or ski-mountaineering. They should have heel grooves for use with a cable binding. They are heavier than the other models, usually stiffer, but warmer at the same time.

The light touring boot

I would recommend the light touring boot for most skiers. There are many models on the market. It is right between the racing boot and touring boot (Photo 12). You can get these in high versions and in rather low versions. The main advantage of the higher boot is its warmth;

it also keeps out the snow better. However, I don't think the higher boot gives a lot more ankle support, since it is not that stiff.

The racing boot

This boot is the track shoe of the x-c world. It's light, flexible to the point of being flimsy—and you'd better move fast if you want to keep your feet warm in them. Obviously, racing boots are designed with one purpose in mind: that is, to suit the racer.

The fit

The most important thing about a boot is its fit. Be sure to try on boots with the socks you plan to wear skiing—perhaps just a pair of knicker socks, or a pair of wool socks and another, lighter pair—and then find a pair of boots that fit like street shoes. Some boots are made on wide lasts and may not fit snugly around the heel. A loose fit here will be the cause of many blisters. Naturally, don't get boots so short that your toes jam into the fronts of them, or else you'll lose your toenails.

   If your boot has a roll of padding or some elastic material along the top around the ankle, this will help keep out the snow.

The sole

The trend in boots is toward a sole of composition like polyurethane. With this you don't have to drill holes in the sole for the pin-binding

13. Again from left: touring boot—composition sole; light touring boot —leather sole; racing boot—composition covering a leather sole.

since the material is just soft enough for the pins to stick into. Polyurethane is also more waterproof and wears better than the traditional leather sole. The only problem comes with the flexibility, for some are either a bit stiff, or they bend too easily in the wrong places.

Leather soles are still being produced and these are good. They do need more care, though, and if you have a pin-binding you're faced with the job of drilling holes in the sole. Yet this shouldn't overwhelm you. Put the boot in the binding, clamp it down, remove the boot and you'll see exactly where to drill.

There are some molded rubber or composition boots on the market. These are waterproof but your feet don't breathe in them; and some of them are not very warm in cold weather. But they are a boon to the family with a bunch of kids to equip because they usually are inexpensive, and they can be worn everywhere—indoors and out. They can also double as downhill boots, so they are worth looking into.

The poles

The pole situation is not complicated. You have a good choice here and usually get what you pay for.

The best poles in the world are made right here in the United States by a man named Scott. They are of airplane metal, weigh only about 15 ounces, have a good whip or flex, and don't break.

From Scott poles you can go through other metal poles, fiberglass, tonkin, or bamboo. The bamboo poles are the most inexpensive and are still used by a vast majority of skiers. They are perfectly good.

There are some items to watch for:

1. Get your poles the right height. Stand on the floor, and the poles should fit comfortably under your armpits.

2. Be sure the pole tip is curved *forward* so that it pulls out of the snow when you ski. Don't get stuck with a straight-tipped Alpine pole unless there is no alternative.

3. If you want, here are a couple of items you can merely get fussy about.

Many skiers prefer a tight-fitting, wide strap for more support. Others like an adjustable strap for use in varying snow depths. If

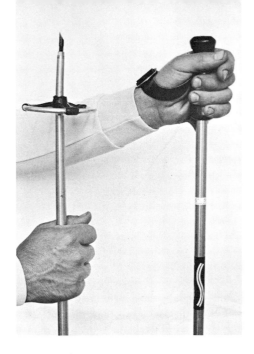

14. The slightly curved tip and the adjustable handle strap are trademarks of x-c poles.

your strap isn't tight fitting you can usually find a way to cinch it by using tape.

Pole grips come in molded plastic, various kinds of leather, or cork. Cork looks nice, feels nice and is usually a bit more expensive.

The pole baskets are of different diameters and materials. The trend is away from leather crosspieces with a wooden ring, and toward rubber or plastic rings. The wider the basket the easier it will be for you to get some push in deep snow. Racers have a packed pole-track and therefore can use a very narrow, light basket. You can imagine how little heft the baskets contribute to poles that weigh less than a pound.

Care of equipment

Veteran racers often spend hours readying their equipment for a big event, because having their skis in top shape is important during a long-distance race. Imagine being able to glide even a half an inch farther in each stride because of a well-kept ski and a superior wax job! Over a 15-kilometer course this really adds up.

The family skier can use all the procedures I describe here, some to a lesser degree, and be relatively free of problems arising from badly kept equipment. They're well worth the effort in savings and efficiency, not to mention pride.

The skis

Let's look at the skis in three different situations: first, when they're new; next, during the season as you are using them; and, finally, when you store them for the summer.

New Skis

Most new wooden skis are sold with a coating of protective varnish or lacquer on the bottoms. This has to come off since it is deathly slow as a substitute for wax, and it doesn't even hold the wax if you try and cover it. I use a combination of a strong, liquid paint remover and elbow grease—the elbow grease to wield a scraper.

The most popular scraper with us is a flat, rectangular steel one made by Stanley. This really has eight edges—each side of the rectangle counts as one, and you can flip it over for four more—which can be

26

sharpened with a file when they get dull. There are lots of scrapers made especially for skis and many of these have rounded sections which are good for scraping the groove. If you don't have a tool for the groove you can round off a corner on a rectangular scraper; or try a sharpened nail head, holding it with a pair of pliers, or a sharpened screw head. We've even shaped and sharpened narrow steel spoons and used them to clean out the groove. Having a groove tool will be helpful in scraping wax off your skis too.

After scraping, the bottoms should be sanded smooth. Then if you want the ultimate in smoothness, polish the bottoms with steel wool. Now they're ready for waxing, which I shall discuss in a separate chapter.

If you have nonwood bottoms they can be prepared quickly by smoothing them with some sandpaper or steel wool. Here is an advantage in having a nonwood bottom: the preparation necessary prior to **waxing** is much simpler than that for wood. But I'll say more about this below.

During the season

During the season the bottoms will get rough again. They get gouged by sharp objects; splinters are likely to appear on wood bottoms; sometimes granular snow is tough on any bottom. If you have plastic, lignostone or hickory edges the bottom surface down the middle occasionally wears down, leaving the harder material in the edges protruding and producing what we call "railing." (When this happens you know either that your wax has not been holding well enough to protect the ski, or that you have been skiing in some very coarse snow conditions. Sometimes it can't be avoided.)

All of these kinds of damage should be corrected by a thorough job of smoothing again. You can be fairly vigorous in scraping wood bottoms: you might get a cup or so of fine shavings. I've seen wood skis scraped so much that the groove is noticeably shallower.

If you're still left with a gouge or hole after this smoothing or scraping, then you should fill the place with plastic wood—that is, if you have a wood bottom. Filling these holes in nonwood isn't so easy. Some epoxies will hold for a while, some Alpine kofix candles might work.

Chalk up one for the wood bottoms: while they take more care, they are easier to repair.

The railing effect I mentioned is serious. The edges behave like runners and make the ski more difficult to turn or slide around—you'll think they are downhill skis, they go so straight. More important, when the ski does slide sideways there is an increased danger of hooking sharp objects in under the edge and tearing off a section of it. If this happens you're in real trouble, and the best thing to do is get a craftsman to cut out this section of your ski and put in a new, little block of wood as a patch.

The sides of the ski should be kept clean. Most people don't scrape the finish off the sides; but after it begins to wear off anyway, it's wise to keep the sides waxed. Common paraffin is fine for this.

The tops get nicked up too, after a while. I never refinish the top, but you might want a different appearance. Again, it's a good idea to keep the tops waxed with paraffin. This serves two purposes: it keeps the snow from building up on your skis so you don't have to carry it along with you, and it helps protect the wood from moisture.

Storing your skis

After the season I think it's best to leave the running wax on the bottoms for summer storage. One theory holds that a wooden ski will better maintain its shape if the stresses resulting from heat and moisture are equal on the tops and bottoms. This is apparently why the skis are lacquered top and bottom at the factory. It wouldn't do to have a bottom, regardless of the material, untreated and exposed to different atmospheric conditions, while the top, because of its finish, remained unaffected. (You probably wouldn't leave one side of a door untreated, unless you wanted it to warp.) Anyway, this is my excuse for not cleaning the klister off my skis in the spring.

I try to store my skis in a cool, dry place, where the temperature won't change radically all the time. And I do *not* block them together. The best reason for not blocking them together and trying to put more camber in them is this, as it was once explained to me: if you can block the skis and put more camber in them, it will be a simple matter to take it out by skiing on them. So, it won't do any good.

Heating the ski

Sometimes it's necessary to use a lot of heat either to apply wax or to clean it off your skis. Occasionally this heat will put some extra camber in wood skis (though the extra bend doesn't last long). If you are satisfied with the camber in your skis and have just finished using a lot

15. This 63-year-old tourskier knows the value of a well-kept ski.

of heat on the bottoms, turn the skis over and heat the tops. This should keep things in balance. But be careful not to burn the finish.

In using a blowtorch of any sort great care should be exercised. I've seen so many skis singed, even charred, by skiers who weren't paying attention. The situation with nonwood bottoms can be worse. Some of these don't just singe or turn black like wood; instead, they start burning! A hole in a synthetic bottom isn't easy to repair.

A few of the first-rank skiers—admittedly perfectionists—keep heat as far away from their skis as possible. They scrape the wax off, and use a wax solvent if they have to, rather than apply heat. Their theory is that the heat damages the wood fibers on the bottoms and thereby makes them rougher and hence slower. And of course it's speed they want.

Ski bindings

Bindings should be mounted so that the toe of the boot is approximately over the balance point of the ski. If your shop has not mounted them for you, use the directions that come with the bindings themselves.

Problems occur when the binding screws loosen. The binding wiggles and the screw holes enlarge. (Have you ever been out in the woods and lost a binding? Good luck!) If the holes get too large, plug them with a wooden matchstick, or some splinters and some glue, and redrill; or plug the holes and move the binding slightly forward or backward to use new wood for the screw holes. If the holes aren't too large but the screws come loose occasionally, plug them with a little steel wool and some matchsticks, then put the screws back in.

However, by keeping the screws tight all the time you can avoid the trouble of such repairs.

If the pin holes in the boot sole get too large you can fill them with epoxy glue and redrill; or get a new leather tip put on the sole to drill; or get a composition tip put on and you won't have to drill at all.

Another problem arises when the boot shrinks slightly and does not fit snug in the binding. Then the boot wiggles and, if you have a pin binding, the holes in the boot are likely to get too large. So check the binding fit carefully. If the boot has shrunk, try hammering in the sides of the binding, or adjusting it if you can. On some bindings this can't be done.

In every case, try and keep a tight fit between the boot and the sides of the binding.

You can actually wax your bindings to keep the snow off. There are also some de-icing compounds which keep ice from forming on the bindings and at the same time keep the moving parts loose.

Ski boots

There isn't much difference between caring for x-c boots and caring for shoes, or other kinds of boots. I use either wax polish or a waterproofing material such as silicone on the whole boot.

> *Warning:* If the boots get wet, dry them slowly. Some boots will crack if you bring them in wet and dry them rapidly on the top of a radiator or heat duct. To help in drying you can fill the insides with some newspaper or other absorbent material.

Ski poles

Two situations can really embarrass you.

One is having the handle strap tear or break. You should be able to notice any weak spots in the strap and tape them, or replace the entire strap. I know straps don't tear very often, but if it ever happens to you I think you'll be amazed how much you depend on the straps.

The other situation is more common, and it's a killer. You guessed it—the basket falls off in the middle of a tour. If you haven't tried skiing in deep snow with a basketless pole you haven't met with one of the ultimates in frustration. So, better to check the cotterpin, wire, or whatever holds your basket on. It's safer to replace the parts once a year than suffer out on the trail.

A molded rubber or plastic basket that slips on over the tip can be replaced easiest by running hot water over the ring, soaping the pole shaft, then sliding it on. Don't impale yourself in the process, but when you make the initial move to get the ring slipping down over the shaft you really have to shove. There's no stopping halfway because you won't make it them.

You ought to use paraffin wax or de-icer on your pole baskets also. If the basket has wood or leather products in it, it's a good idea to protect them from moisture. More important, wax helps keep the snow off the basket and makes lifting poles easier.

For travel

The competitors who fly around the world have always packed their skis and poles in ski bags for ease of transporting. Now, ski bags are becoming popular everywhere for travel by car, bus or train, and I strongly recommend them. They are easy to attach to a car ski rack, hold lots of equipment, and protect the skis from all that junk that flies up off the road during winter travel.

They're easy to make. Get the nearest seamstress—your wife, mother, sister or girl friend will do—to sew up some tough denim or heavy sailcloth, leave one end open for packing, put a carrying handle (or reinforced strap of the material, of convenient length) lengthwise near the middle where the balance is best for you, and you're all set. Or, you can buy them.

The clothes for it

Clothing is another instance of how everybody can fit into the x-c scene. The range of what you can wear is so great as almost to be unbelievable. The U.S. racers have their own little outfits that are a uniform: dark stretch knickers, light tops, white socks. The tourskiers who try to dress like tourskiers have theirs. Then there are the skiers who wear what they want to

It's a very low-key thing, this matter of how to dress. Almost anything goes as long as it has some element of practicality.

There are a few tips I can give you that might avoid some uncomfortable situations. After that, you're on your own.

The clothing market is opening up in North America. It's safe to say that, at this writing, the manufacturers are producing so many different styles and colors that the United States is the world leader in the variety of clothes for x-c. The traditionalists may not cotton to the new designs—which include wild colors and one-piece suits—but they're here to stay. So, as with equipment, if you look around long enough you will probably be able to find anything that fits your needs.

Things to keep in mind

Before actually itemizing the clothing there are a few general remarks that should be made.

Loose and easy. If you are fairly vigorous in your skiing, you should avoid clothing that will bind you. For instance, Alpine stretch pants are out. Shirts or tops that might bind you in the shoulders, or behind your shoulders, are out.

32

16 & 17. More of the leeway in x-c: the youngster at left does his own thing, compared with the U.S. Team "uniform" at right.

Breathing. Clothing such as nylons which do not breathe are not too satisfactory. If you perspire very much and you can't get rid of this moisture, sooner or later you will be cold and clammy.

> *Note:* I won't say any more about wind-chill, etc., than this: You should be aware of the fact that wind on a cold day can be very tough on you, even dangerous. You should have a chart available to study for windy, cold weather and you should be careful of prolonged exposure during conditions like this. Using vaseline to rub on exposed parts like the face is O.K., but it will not protect you from frostbite in all conditions.

Weight. Heavy clothing simply isn't necessary if you are going to be moving around enough to generate heat to stay warm. You don't have to dress as if you're in for a long chair-lift ride to the top of some peak.

We don't have a very warm house in winter—it's kept at around 65 F.—and I can wear about the same amount of clothing on a tour that I do sitting around inside during snowtime. Actually, since I'm so often suited up in x-c clothes, it's an easy matter to grab my hat and gloves, step out the back door, and take off. (That brings up another point: lots of x-c clothing is nicely geared for general wear around and about.)

So forget the quilted parka, the mackinaw and those heavy sweaters for skiing, and save them for afterwards in case you'll be standing around or having a long drive home before you can change.

On a tour, it's better to take a couple of light shirts, skiing with the extra one tied around your waist until you need it. I would also go with light knickers, and then use long underwear on those cold days when you will really be glad to have it on.

Hats and earbands

Anyone who exercises quite a bit knows that his head gives off a lot of heat. When I ski, I like a hat or an earband that will soak up some of the sweat, because the more sweat I can keep out of my eyes, the better. At the same time it's important to have material in your headgear that will breathe. You've probably seen skiers come in after a long workout, their hats covered with hoarfrost. This has come from their little old heads, and has just frozen on there.

On real warm days you might not need a hat. If it's mildly cold, you might get away with an earband. If it's very cold, you might want both an earband *and* a hat. This is a very good combination for bitter weather.

Don't be afraid to overdress in the hat division. There isn't any problem to tucking an extra earband or hat into your pocket, and it might come in very handy for a long, downhill run following a warm climb.

Shirts and tops

As I have mentioned, for x-c the most important qualities are lightness and the ability to let the moisture evaporate. A T-shirt or a cotton turtleneck or a fishnet—each is good. But if you cover these with a nylon shirt you are likely to get pretty uncomfortable. I cover my undershirt with a so-called running top made of a knit material called crepe. It's a stretch fabric and therefore doesn't bind. It also breathes.

In most instances I use just the crepe top (which has a pocket) and a turtleneck. If it's warm out, either the turtleneck or the top will do fine alone. If it's cold and I'm going on an extended tour I might take along an extra windbreaker—a light one—wrapped around my waist. If you start to get cold you can always move faster and warm up.

Gloves

Well, my favorites gloves are still those cotton work jobbies affectionately known in Eastern racing circles as "French-Canadien racing gloves." Since writing the first edition, the price of these beauties has risen from 39 cents, but I still find them the best buy on the market. You can go whole hog and get real, ventilated, Finnish racing gloves for around $11.00, and there are lots of in-betweens. (Some racers have used handball gloves. These breathe—they're full of holes!)

There are lots of mittens addicts. But I prefer the gloves because they give you a much better feel for the poling action. However, there's no question that mittens are warmer.

In very cold weather some skiers vaseline their hands, or use some talcum powder. I'm not sure this helps. Another trick is to wear a pair of silk gloves as liners under another pair of gloves or mittens.

If you're desperate for gloves or mittens some day, pull on a pair of socks over your hands. They're better than nothing at all.

Knickers and pants

Knickers are the traditional x-c pants. They allow the most freedom of movement, and, if you have knicker socks along with them, your legs don't scuff as they pass each other in the stride. For knickers, I would get light ones. Then, if it's cold, get an old pair of long underwear and cut off the legs just above the knees. This is just perfect for those bitter, windy days.

Warm-up pants are becoming more popular. These were brought in by the racing crowd and were used primarily to warm up in before a race, and to stay warm in after a race. Immediately before a race they were shed in favor of the knickers. Now, since warm-ups feel so good,

18. A variety of warm-up clothes. Author, wearing crutches (an injury from soccer, not x-c), sheepskin hat, parka and "moon" boots, and two of his sons, who are sporting Alpine pants they'll shed for racing.

lots of skiers use them instead of knickers. If they are fairly snug around the lower leg they don't allow any scuffing. And, if you're going to stand around a lot, as coaches do, they're better than straight knickers, being warmer. Wear 'em myself.

These are traditional items, remember. But—while I wouldn't recommend bell bottoms—lots of other combinations are possible. If it's warm, shorts are just great. Or you can try the Putney "springtime uniform." This is long underwear with shorts on top. It's very fast on the downhills because there is so little wind resistance. I haven't seen many x-c'ers in leotards, but they would be fastest of all!

Socks

If you have knickers you're sort of bound to use knicker socks. If you don't, you'll get mighty cold. Wool socks are the best since they are warm and shed the snow very well. There are other lighter, tighter-fitting socks and you pay the price for this lightness. You don't stay as warm, but if that's not a problem, O.K.

These days, most of the racers wear their second pair of socks, if they wear them at all, inside their knicker socks. The skiers on my team chide me when I wear mine outside. It dates me, they say. That's the way it is. When I want to look older and wiser, I wear them outside.

If you're wearing long pants and don't need knicker socks, you should try the so-called thermal socks. I've had good luck with them.

I've seen some skiers wrap a plastic freezer bag over their socks before the boot goes on. If they're going out in real wet weather, or know they're going to get wet feet, they claim this helps.

Avoiding cold, wet feet

It's easy to get wet feet, and this is the complaint I hear most about. Skiers' feet can even sweat enough to get socks and boots wet, to say nothing of the snow and other elements working on one's feet from the outside. There are a few precautions you can take to help avoid this problem.

1. Gaiters are becoming very popular. These fit over the top of your boot at the ankle. The biggest job they do, I think, is to keep the snow from going down inside your boot. Snow seeping in here is the surest way to get wet feet. So, if you're going to be skiing in deep snow a lot, you should invest in a pair of gaiters. They come in many sizes, from very narrow on up to knee length.

2. There are some boot-gloves on the market too. They are made of a rubberized material and keep your boots dry. You can slip them on and wear them satisfactorily in most pin-bindings.

3. Another, and inexpensive, way to keep your feet warm is to put on a pair of old tight-fitting socks right over your boots. In most cases you can wear these with your ski bindings.

It goes without saying that if you want to have warm feet you have to keep your boots dry. Polish them regularly, or use waterproofing compounds.

Then, when you step out your door to go skiing, stand still a minute or two and allow your boots to cool off. If you rush right out into the snow with warm boots, the snow will melt and you'll be on your way toward wet feet.

19. *The Cliff Montagne family at Winter Park, Colorado, set out for a jaunt, with a picnic for three in Dad's fanny pack.*

After skiing

The best thing to do after a tour is to dry off and keep' warm. If you have a shower and a change of clothing available, that's fine. If you don't, and you're stuck somewhere, there are a couple of things you can do.

I suppose the most welcome item after a workout is a dry T-shirt. If you can bring one of these along with you, jump right into it. You might even want to rub yourself off with snow first. It's very refreshing.

If you don't have any extra clothing to change into, try this. Switch the order of your shirts. Sometimes the outside shirt is the driest and you can put that on right next to your skin. Put the wet one on the outside and maybe that will dry soon, too.

Odds and ends

Until recently, the use of goggles in x-c has always been considered a No-No. The problem used to be that the goggles steamed up so much that you couldn't see out of them.

But now they've improved the ventilation system enough on some models to make fogging no longer a problem. At any rate a few skiers are using them. I know we were all amazed to see photographs of Finland's top woman, Marjatta Kajosmaa, racing with goggles in a snowstorm at Holmenkollen, Norway, in 1971. She won. And maybe now all the Finnish girls are sporting goggles.

If the sun is very bright and you're going to be out a long time, you could wear goggles with dark lenses to protect your eyes. *Sunglasses are better,* however, and I would recommend them, especially in the spring when the sun gets higher and brighter. You might invest in one of those elastic bands that go around the back of the head to keep the glasses from slipping off when you're really moving.

A nice item to have is a *fanny pack*—also called a kidney pack—a shaped pouch that straps around your waist and is worn out of the way below the small of your back. You can put extra wax, corks, snacks, socks, etc., in one of these and carry it along with ease on your outings. They come in several sizes.

Technique

As I mentioned in the beginning, I hope technique is not something that's going to bug you. The most fun in x-c skiing is moving around the terrain any way you like, and personal enjoyment should be your most important consideration. However, I feel there are many skiers who like to work on their technique and this chapter is written for them. I am describing racing form here, but this just happens to be the most efficient way to ski. If you are a family skier and want to work at it, I'm sure you can learn to go fast over certain sections of the track and get that thrill of speed which comes easily with the proper technique. I figure there's nothing wrong with trying to mimic the hotshots.

If you want to do your own thing and ski your own way, just skip this chapter and no one will be the loser. I'm serious about this.

Faster, sooner

Although the approach for skiing on the flat which I used in the 1964 version of this book is still perfectly valid, over the past seven years I've developed a slightly different emphasis, and it's this new departure that I'm going to describe. Ideally, the effect is the same; actually, however, I've found that my new approach seems to get more satisfactory results sooner. But if you don't like this new approach, go back and use the earlier editions.

Skiing x-c is closely related to walking. For one thing, your arms and legs alternate. By this I mean that as you walk, or ski, your left arm and right leg come forward together, then your right arm and left leg. Did you ever notice this? For another, the faster you walk, or ski, the more you stretch out in your movements. Also, when you walk or ski uphill, you tend to lean forward more and usually shorten your stride. There are other connections between walking and skiing, but I think you can see my point without them.

20. Pretty good form for a 15-year-old racer. Note the drive in that forward knee, complete extension of arm and leg to the rear, rear foot close to the snow. The right hand might be too close to the face.

Behind then, in front now

When skiers in this country first became technique-conscious, largely as a result of a movie put out by Rick Eliot in the 1950's, the emphasis on the diagonal technique—this skiing stride where your arms and legs alternate—was put on the *kick*. The skiers were taught to kick down on the track and backwards, then to relax this kicking leg in preparation for bringing it forward for the next stride. (Some were even taught to lift the rear leg slightly: these days you will occasionally see a skier who is kicking his rear leg high, hanging it out there to dry. For efficient skiing, this wastes effort and breaks momentum—and hence is wrong.)

Now, though, my main emphasis in teaching this diagonal technique is on what happens out in front of the skier. Here is the key to the difference in approach.

Don't ask me to defend my comments on good technique by citing principles from physics—vectors and stuff like that. All I can say is that this material has been arrived at after thousands of hours of coaching, practicing myself, skiing with others, and discussions. Maybe a physicist will come along some day and analyze these movements, using mathematical formulae and other knowledge at his disposal, and tell me scientifically what I'm doing. Meanwhile . . .

One, two, three

This chapter is in three major sections, with sideline comments. First I'll cover flat skiing, then uphill skiing, and finally, downhill.

I think with some practice many of you will be able to display technique used by the world's best racers. The only difference between you and them is a little matter of conditioning. (And *that's* the understatement of the week. Those hotdogs can get cranked up and ski at full speed for more than 30 miles.)

> *Note:* In working on technique you will need a good track to practice in. Without it you will not be able to ski effectively. (See the chapter on Tour Races for track-setting comments.) You should also be waxed fairly well if you want to work on technique. Waxing is important enough to be covered in a separate chapter.
>
> Therefore, in talking about technique from here on, I'll assume you're properly waxed and have a good track.

Skiing on the flat

There are two basic methods for skiing along the flats, and no matter how many different names you hear them called by, don't get confused. They're simple:

> 1. You can use some form of *double-poling.* This is poling with both arms simultaneously, either using single steps or keeping your skis parallel, like sled runners.

21. *Diagonal stride again, with the right-hand pole going in directly opposite the left (driving) foot.*

2. You can use *diagonal* technique (or, as it's often called, the *single stride* or *single stick*). The diagonal comes from the use simultaneously of one arm, say the left, and the opposite leg, in this case the right.

Anyway, the diagonal method is as basic as can be. It's used 90 percent of the time, and is really *the* x-c stride. (To a modified extent, it's even used in most uphill skiing.) So if you can master this you've come a long way toward getting the maximum return for your x-c effort.

Diagonal (single stride)

I'll put you in an extended diagonal stride position. This is the position you see the most pictures of. We'll say your weight is on the right leg, it is slightly bent, and the left arm is forward. Your right arm and your left leg are to the rear, with the left foot slightly off the snow. You should carry yourself leaning forward at the waist . . .

(Now, while you are standing there on one leg, is a good time to point out the matter of counterbalances. The more you lean over at the waist and the more you drive that right leg and left arm forward, the further back you must extend that right arm and left leg—or else you'll tip over forward, like a toppling statue. Under most conditions, the top skiers extend themselves quite a bit. This takes strength, especially in the legs, and good balance. If you are a beginner don't expect to achieve this extended position your first few times on skis. You probably won't have the balance, even if you are strong enough.)

Power from that forward knee

. . . Let's begin skiing. To do this, simply drive your left leg forward along with your right arm. If you emphasize the drive of the forward knee, the left in this case, you'll find yourself gliding along on your left leg, with your right arm forward, and your other arm and leg extended to the rear. That's about all there is to the diagonal technique, except for the poling motion: as you drive your left leg forward you should be pushing backward in the snow with your left pole. You can see how it's all put together in Photo 20.

This forward knee-drive is so important. Its power separates the good—i.e., effective—skiers from the others.

Many a skier drives forward, but, as his legs pass each other, he relaxes and discontinues the knee-drive. There is not as much power or extension there, and such skiers will not go so fast. This kind of skiing is often telegraphed by the arm movements or body position. If the body is upright, chances are the forward knee-drive is insufficient. If the arms come forward with elbows bent sharply or don't go backward beyond the hip, their shortened swing is proof that the extension is not complete.

Where the poles come in

Use of the poles is important, but you should keep everything in perspective. If you think that arms contribute so much power to the stride, compared to the legs, try—as I tell some of my skiers—walking around all day on your hands.

The poling motion in the diagonal technique should be loose and rhythmical, fairly well extended to the front and to the rear, and timed to coincide with the knee-drive forward—that is, as your knee drives ahead you should be pushing back with the arm and pole on that same side. Clearly, you can get the best forward thrust if you push back with your arm close to your body, and not out to the side so that the pole basket is too far from your ski. And the pole will have to be shoved in the snow directly opposite your driving foot, and slanted to the rear, as in Photo 21. (If you set it in ahead and slanted forward you'll surely be working against yourself if you push.)

In putting on your poles, slip your hand up through the strap and then grip the handle (look back at Photo 14). This way the strip will offer support on the palm of your hand as you push with the pole.

Holding the pole firmly at all times will tire you quickly, though, so you'll find it easy and natural to loosen your grip—letting go with all but your thumb and index finger—as it is thrust to the rear.

Diagonal summary

A good basic rule to follow in using the diagonal stride is this:

Try to make all your movements directly ahead. Use economy of motion, by making only the movements which contribute to carrying you in the direction of the track. In other words, don't bob at the waist, don't bend sideways at the waist, don't bring your arms across in front of your body, don't lift your rear leg high, don't hop or jump up and down.

If you feel after a while that you're being too mechanical, don't worry. You'll develop some little stylistic flourishes that will distinguish you from an automaton. For instance, I seem to cross one arm in front of my body, but not the other; and we have one boy on the U.S. Team who runs with his head cocked to the side.

Common faults and how to correct them

Not enough knee-drive forward, or not enough extension. To improve, you may have to develop more strength and balance. Skiing is the best way to do this. You can try skiing occasionally without poles. This helps the balance.

For extension, concentrate on driving the front arm out straight

—e.g., reaching forward with your pole without bending your arm. Although most skiers don't use a straight arm out front, this sometimes is helpful in getting better extension.

Upper-body bob. If someone watches you ski from the side he can tell how much motion of the upper body you have. As the better skiers glide along the flats their heads stay at just about the same height from the track all the time. Others bounce up and down in their strides and eventually wear themselves out—or get sore backs.

To eliminate this bob, try relaxing your back, even to consciously rounding your shoulders slightly at the end of your glide or forward knee-drive.

Side-bending. This could be a balance problem, and it's easy to spot by having someone sight on you from directly ahead or behind. Sometimes if the tracks are too close together, or you are skiing too much on your edges instead of on the flat of your ski, you will bend from side to side with each stride.

Sometimes it happens because you swing your arms too wide, instead of straight ahead. Skiing without poles will often remedy this situation.

Hanging the rear leg out to dry. If you ski with a fast tempo (and we're coming to tempo in a moment), there is hardly time to leave that leg out there, to the rear. So if you're one of those fellows who lift their rear leg too high, try skiing with a faster tempo. It also will help if you concentrate on keeping the rear foot as close to the snow as possible. This in turn can be helped by pointing the rear hand downward toward the snow as you finish your poling motion.

Refinements for the racer

Tempo. I have just mentioned using a higher tempo as a method to help correct the high, rear-leg lift. Tempo is very important and it's "stepping up the beat" that separates the men from the boys. You might be able to do everything that a top skier can do, except that your movements are just a bit slower. Well, you know who wins *that* race.

Skiing at extremely high tempo takes a lot of practice. We often run

22. *Only practice will bring such smoothness, power and extension as this at extremely high tempo.*

sprints on skis for 200 yards or so. This is an all-out effort and one would never go quite this fast in a race unless it was right at the finish. In doing sprints like this the tendency is to tighten up or get tired pretty quickly—at least after a short distance. The best remedy is for you to analyze your movements and work on skiing in as relaxed a way as you can.

It sounds crazy, but often the drawback to a high tempo is the arm motion. You'll find that you can complete the leg's part of each stride faster than you can the arm's part. Therefore if you find your tempo is too slow you may have to ease up on the arm stroke a bit. (As I say, always: the power comes from the legs anyway.)

When you learn to ski at high tempo in the effortlessly powerful manner of Photo 22, then you're ready for the big time.

Which snow, which tempo

That's not all there is to it, though. On some snow conditions it's better to use different tempos and different forces in your stride. For instance, on slow snow, you can drive forward with all your power but you won't be skiing very efficiently: the snow is simply slowing you down too fast with the suction in each stride, considering the amount of effort you put into it.

A good general rule is this: On high-speed snows, your tempo is slightly slower than on slow snows. On slow snows, a higher tempo is called for, but you don't put quite as much effort into each stride; also, try to maintain a fairly fast, even speed along the flats.

On faster snow on the flat, your over-all speed would be greater, but it would tend to vary more within each stride. This is why: Immediately after your leg-drive forward you will reach your peak speed—but, since the resulting glide would be a bit longer, you'll decelerate more before you come to the end of it. For instance—and these figures are approximate—on fast snow your top speed in one stride might be 12 miles per hour, slowing to 8 mph before the next leg-drive; on slow snow your top speed might very well be only 10 mph, yet you couldn't afford the time to let it decelerate lower than 8 mph. Thus, in this hypothetical case you have a deceleration of 4 mph on fast snow, and 2 mph on slow snow.

So a fast-snow speed graph, which considers each stride, would wave up and down a bit. The speed graph for slower snow would be steadier, because of less driving effort, yet higher tempo.

Riding your skis

How is the weight carried forward in the x-c stride?

Is there a sudden thrust followed by a static position during the glide forward? Or, have you got the picture of a runner driving his leg forward and then remaining inert on his skis, like a statue? That's what the majority of skiers do.

But I prefer something different. I'm more impressed when the initial sudden drive is sustained as the knee and leg continue to drive forward, and when body dynamics are used during the stride to keep the motion going forward faster.

Under certain favorable conditions, the good skier will be able to use some body dynamics—and he's the one who gets that extra inch or so out of each stride. The gain is not because he holds his stride longer, but because he rides a better ski.

Let me see if I can amplify.

Have you ever ski-jumped? You spring off the take-off, you're airborne—— And what do you do out there? (Cry for help? No!) The better jumpers continue to stretch, or drive. Some think of pulling themselves through the air with their shoulders, or leading with their heads. They get more distance in their jumps than the fellows who go out there and just hang, like a sack of potatoes.

You say you haven't jumped. O.K., how about Alpine skiing? If you're experienced in it, you know that, when you make a turn, you don't get maximum results if you set your edges and "statue" through the rest of the turn. You've learned what a difference it makes if some sort of power movement, weighting or unweighting, is continued throughout the turn.

So, in the x-c stride, if you can carry some sort of slight body effort forward during the gliding phase, you will be skiing with an effective difference. The extra pressure might come from the upper body, or the arms, or the legs, especially the upper leg.

Well, work on it if you want to. There aren't many skiers who do it to perfection; but as I've said, if you can gain even half an inch a stride, you're really in the clover.

Double-poling

Even though the single stride with diagonal poling is used most of the time you'll want to practice your double-poling for certain conditions. On gradual downhill sections of terrain, or on fast icy snow, on flat parts of the trail, or before making step turns (discussed below), the double-pole is a fairly easy, natural maneuver.

You can begin by standing still on the flat, skis held parallel, and pushing off with your poles simultaneously. As in the single-poling action, be sure the pole baskets are always pointed to the rear. You can get a good idea of your arm strength by propelling yourself along a flat stretch this way. (See the Training chapter for poling drills.)

If you are coasting down a hill and want to increase your speed you can also double-pole. This is good terrain to learn the poling motion on, and to strengthen your arms and shoulders.

The most common double-pole follows from the single stride. To get into this, bring both arms forward in the single stride, and pole with them simultaneously (Photo 23). The success you have with this double-poling stride will depend on your balance and your strength. Some strong skiers with good balance almost throw themselves out over the lead ski, both arms reaching forward, and then give a tremendous

23. Starting to double-pole from the single–diagonal–stride.

thrust with the poling motion by using their arms, shoulders and body weight. Others will not have the balance to venture so far forward.

The poling motion, if it is strong, will have a good follow-through (Photo 24).

There are lots of variations of double-poling as used by individual good skiers, but it would take too much space to describe them here. Work out whichever modification suits your style and strength.

One good hint I can give, though, is that you try and get your body weight into the poling motion. This means not pushing too hard until your arms are bent—and then, when they are bent, sort of sinking down on the poles with your weight as you push.

Uphill skiing

Skiing uphill under your own steam is one of the trademarks of the x-c skier. Here is a place where many of the unique features of x-c combine to give you a great deal of satisfaction. The equipment is light and allows that freedom of movement which is necessary for almost all uphill skiing. The practiced x-c'er, I dare say, is a trifle stronger than his Alpine counterpart, and therefore able to exert a bit more strength to get up hills with ease. And, finally, the proper wax provides that extra in grip, or purchase, which enables you to go straight up some of the fairly steep slopes (Photo 25).

24. Double-pole completed. Pole handles are cradled momentarily in the palms of the hands, guided slightly by thumbs and index fingers.

There are almost as many different ways to ski uphill as there are degrees of steepness. The good skier uses different techniques with varying amounts of effort, depending on the slope. I'll hit on six or seven of the methods.

Diagonal stride

If the uphill slope is relatively flat and your wax is good, and if there's a good track and you're feeling strong, you can glide up the hill using the plain, old, on-the-flat, diagonal technique. To get some glide going uphill takes quite a bit of strength, and sometimes it's helpful to assume a slightly crouched body position. Be careful not to sit back though; failing to keep the body weight forward is one of the most common faults of skiers going uphill.

Bounding stride

If the slope is steeper—but not so steep that you have to sidestep or herringbone (see below)—there are two techniques that may serve. One is a bounding stride used by racers when they're in a hurry. They practically leap from one ski forward on to the other. The amount of extension depends on the slope, the skier's strength and his wax; but in general he extends less than in his diagonal stride on the flat.

25. Straight up! Body weight forward, good wax and a bit of extra strength.

Dog-trot

The other method, which I'll call the dog-trot, is good for fairly steep slopes. In this one you lean forward a bit more, assume a fairly low body position, and take rather short steps.

The key to this dog-trot is a "soft" ski out front. By that, I mean you cushion the step by bending the ankle and the knee. The knee should be right over, or even ahead of, the foot. It's as if you're *sneaking* up the hill, or you're trotting along on a bunch of fresh eggs, trying not to break them. *It's important to keep your body weight forward.* If you get back on your heels and have to rock forward on to the ball of your foot in each step, you'll soon get tired.

The poles should be used with a minimum effort. If it is necessary to pole hard with each step, or to hold yourself from slipping with each step, then (*a*) you should be using another technique, or (*b*) you need more wax, or (*c*) your weight is back too far, or (*d*) you're not doing it right in the first place. The poles are almost an afterthought.

Another way of thinking about it is to imagine yourself running, or dog-trotting, up an inclined cement ramp, with sneakers on. If you wanted to jog up the ramp in the most relaxed manner, how would you do it? Chances are you'd dog-trot.

Sidestep

The sidestep is a sure, easy way to climb. Stand with your skis across the slope, or at right angles to the fall-line. (The fall-line is the route a

26. The sidestep takes plenty of time, but it gets you there.

ball would take if it could roll freely and unimpeded down the hill, and so this is the most direct way up a slope.)

Then lift the uphill ski and move it up the hill a foot or so, digging in the uphill edge as you put it down. Now lift the other ski, place it beside the upper one—and you should be a little closer to the top of the hill (Photo 26). Continue.

Traverse

The traverse is probably the tourskier's most common method of getting up hills. It is really nothing more than a single stride with a bit of the sidestep effect thrown in.

Skiing up a slope with linked traverses is similar to taking a zigzag road to the top of a mountain. To start traversing, get crossways to the fall-line and, as you move your uphill ski forward in the single stride, slide it slightly up the hill; then slide the other ski alongside and ahead. Thus you proceed forward across the slope and upward at the same time. The poling motion is identical with the single stride.

To link one traverse with another, use a herringbone turn—or better still, a kick turn—to change your direction and start across the slope again.

Herringbone

The herringbone is a very quick, but tiring, method of getting up a hill.

The legs and arms alternate, exactly as in the diagonal, but there are

27. The herringbone—a good, fast, energetic way to climb.

some important differences. First, there's no glide (unless you're a superman!); second, your skis are splayed out in a V—or herringbone—pattern, hence the name; third, in order to hold from slipping, you must dig in the inside edge of each ski.

If you're strong and in a hurry, there it is. (It is a very important racing technique, since many of the hills on a competition course are so steep. The U.S. Team even has dry-land drills for this one.)

And when all else fails . . .

As a last resort, you can always take your skis off and walk. Don't laugh. I've been in races when I was so tired and my wax was so bad that I know my times would have been faster if I'd taken off my skis and walked. I would have been disqualified of course, so I grunted it.

But you don't have to keep 'em on. You're out for fun, and x-c is your own thing. Right?

Downhill skiing

There are really two basic situations you'll come up against with your downhill skiing. Either you may be on a trail, following some sort of packed track that doesn't give you much room for choice, or you may be out on your own on an untracked hillside, where you can use lots of different ways to get down.

I'll cover trail skiing first.

The trail: straight down

The fastest, easiest way is straight down. Assume a relaxed, upright position, with weight evenly distributed on both skis, keep flat-footed, and go. If you want some extra speed you can crouch over and rest your forearms on the tops of your knees, as in Photo 28. This tuck cuts down wind resistance and also is restful. Be careful of this position when the slope is bumpy, however, because it's hard to hold then. Better to straighten up.

It's possible to go very fast on x-c skis. In races, on some steep downgrades, x-c skiers get going at least 40 mph, but you can be sure they've got their eye on a nice outrun at the bottom. I'm not recommending such speed for you. In addition, *you should always be able to see your outrun when you're going straight down a hill.* Otherwise you may be headed for trouble and not know it.

Because it's no good to take a chance on bumping into something like a tree or another skier, you'll need a few other methods of controlling your speed and direction of travel. Like the following.

LET YOUR KIDS DO THEIR THING TOO

Whenever parents ask me how to teach pre-teen children how to ski x-c, I always answer, "Leave 'em alone." Simply getting them out on snow for some fun is the best thing you can do—the main idea being that if their parents and friends enjoy skiing, the kids will too. Most youngsters are so loose and are such good mimics that it's hardly necessary to give them formal lessons. Just let them watch some good skiers in action and you'll be surprised at how much they learn. It is important to expose them to good skiers now and then, since they usually pick up what they see: that's why I advise some parents to ski behind, not in front of, their children.

And maybe you can get some bits of good technique from them sometimes. I know I've learned a lot through watching kids who've never had lessons.

28. *Downhill crouch for easy terrain. Some skiers prefer not to cross hands.*

The trail: step turn

The step, or skate, turn is the most efficient method of changing direction in any kind of skiing on any kind of skis. Just raise one ski slightly off the snow, point it in the direction you want to go, set it down, lift the other and bring it alongside the first. (Photo 29)

Naturally, the faster you are going the faster you have to move those skis. In fact, some x-c runners often practice high-speed turns by jumping off the snow with both skis and landing with them pointed in a different direction. This can be difficult, but it's a very neat way to change direction.

The trail: snowplow turn

Snowplowing is possible under most conditions and it has the advantage of being more controlled than straight downhill skiing: you control not only your speed, but also your direction.

In doing the straight-down snowplow, be sure to keep the tips of your skis fairly close together while pushing your ski tails apart to get that edging or braking action. To turn from this position, weight or push harder on one ski, and this force will drive you around in the desired direction.

There are a couple of more informal ways to slow down which I'll cover in a minute. Meanwhile let's hit the open slopes.

29. *The beginning of a step turn.*

Open slope: traversing down

Naturally, you can use all the turns mentioned so far when you have a whole hillside to yourself. And there's a special beauty also. With so much more freedom of movement here, you can lay your own course between and around obstacles, and there are no compulsory corners.

Absolutely the most pleasurable way I know of for going downhill in open terrain is by using the traverse. I like to head down at an angle just steep enough to keep me going. This way, I get the maximum distance out of the slope in return for whatever climb I made up to the start of the downhill piece. I recommend it as effortless, ideal for easy step-turning, and giving you the bonus of time to enjoy the scenery as you go. And it's so quiet that you can often sneak up on animals.

(A friend of mine has developed a technique that's probably unique among ardent x-c'ers for negotiating some of the slopes around Vermont. He is an acrophobiac of the first order and, short of going downhill blindfolded, has perfected the bush-grab. Carefully he gauges his speed so that, when he gets near enough to the first bush on his course, he can grab it and come to a stop. He then heads off for the next bush or tree. After a trip through tree country he comes in covered with twigs and birchbark, happy as a pup with two tails.)

Open slope: Telemark turn

The telemark turn is very graceful and most appropriate for powder

30. In the middle of a Telemark, the classic x-c turn. Note arms used for balance, the advanced right ski's stemming, or turning, effort.

skiing. It was developed long before the present-day Alpine bindings and boots appeared—and in fact long before the resort slopes were packed out with such maddening efficiency. Here's one you just can't do with Alpine equipment. You need that heel-lifting freedom you get with x-c gear.

The turn itself has about gone out of style but I think it ought to be revived. It's a nice test of balance, as shown in Photo 30.

To do it, slide one ski ahead of the other as you go downhill. Slide it so that the binding of the forward ski is about alongside the tip of the following ski. Then stem the forward ski—to the *left* if it's your right ski that is ahead—weight it or edge it slightly, use your arms for balance, and you should go around. Bring your skis together to complete the turn.

Don't worry if you fall. It happens all the time. But after you master this turn and can link them together going down a slope, you will be something to behold.

The turn can be done at very slow speeds. At higher speeds it's a bit more difficult. And, as I said, it's great for powder skiing.

Good anywhere: sit-down and fall

Since writing the first book I have heard of very few broken-bone accidents in x-c skiing—one in particular being a collision between two skiers. But bone breaks are still very rare. Usually the equipment breaks before a leg gets enough stress to do so. This is a marvelous safety feature in x-c, because new skis are a lot cheaper than doctors' fees.

The sit-down

If you get in trouble downhill, don't be too proud to sit down and scoot on your fanny to a stop. Start by easing your weight down so you can drag your hands in the snow on each side—like twin stabilizers—to keep from tipping over sideways. Then gradually let your body sink into the snow.

The fall

I have received lots of comments about my controlled—or uncontrolled?—fall which received photo coverage in the first edition of this book. But I stand (or fall) as before: I did it, I still do it, and it's still fun.

If you find yourself in the middle of an unpremeditated fall, and the landing area is soft, try to save your skis. The preferred fall is one in which the skis pass backwards under the body, do not dig into the snow, and don't break. Some call it the "spread eagle"; in other circles it's described as a belly-whopper.

So I present another picture of an unposed fall for this new edition. In it, two of my sons were teasing each other when they should have been in formation for a scenic, powdery, typically Vermont-y downhill shot. No injuries to bodies or skis in this one either.

31. And I'll say it again . . . (it's fun).

Waxing

This business of waxing is one area that really separates the Nordic from the Alpine. How many Alpine recreational skiers wax every time they go out? Not many. How many tourskiers go out *without* wax? Not many, I venture to say.

In addition, it's always cause for wonderment that an x-c'er can put wax on so he can ski straight up a slope and then, at the top, be able to turn around and ski down without sticking. But if you have ever had good wax, you know that it really does work this way.

Time to confess

Frankly, when I wrote that first book, I spent a great deal of effort trying to simplify waxing procedures in order to attract a crowd, as the fella says (and I'm not sure my simplification attracted throngs to x-c skiing). Anyway, now it can be told: waxing can be difficult.

Of all the mental challenges I have faced, I think trying to decide the wax before a big race, such as an Olympic event, is the greatest. There are so many factors that go into making a decision! Besides that, the pressure is fantastic. I usually try to search back in my memory for a day with similar conditions, and start there.

I feel that there is an increasing number of skiers who want to experiment and learn more about wax. I hope this whole business will always maintain some mystique, however—if only because it gives all x-c'ers an unfailing topic of conversation. There's still another benefit: to hit on the right wax is a thrill in itself. Things you work hard for and succeed at are the most satisfying, and this holds true for waxing.

Enough of that, though. Let's get *you* started.

If you're fairly new at waxing for x-c, I know perfectly well what

32. Share the challenge and you share the fun—even in waxing.

will happen more and more. You'll go out touring with a friend and notice that he's going straight up the hills while you have to herringbone; then on the downhill sections he will coast away from you. You'll not make much of it at the moment, but after the tour you'll ask casually, "Say, ol' buddy, what did you wax for today?" After he tells you, you'll hop down to your supplier and pick up a tube of that stuff, for sure.

There's nothing wrong with this. Don't feel bad. Just be prepared next time.

Which brand?

Writing "how-to" on waxing is an author's nightmare. At least in the past, wax companies have added new waxes yearly, or changed the color-coding regularly. No sooner does the author get a chart figured out than the colors change.

I have heard that some companies are experimenting to find a few special waxes that will work in Japan during the 1972 Olympics. Maybe the salt air will affect the snow and they are trying to get something for their national skiers that no one else has. We'll know after the Games.

The cardinal rule is to learn how to use one brand of wax well, then if you want to expand your supply, move on and learn another brand. Your choice of brand should be dictated in part by the ones which you can obtain easily. It's possible to get hold of about ten brands if you look far enough.

On the U.S. Team we have decided to stick with four brands. We have to limit ourselves somewhere along the line. Since each brand has around ten different waxes we have to worry about only 40 waxes! (We use Rex, Rode, Swix and Ex-Elit; but there are plenty of other good waxes—it's just that we've been able to get hold of these four without much trouble.)

I have a private theory on waxing which you might want to try some day, especially if you get into the situation of using more than one brand. Here it is:

If you are skiing in a country where a particular wax brand is made, lean toward that brand. It's been designed for that country's conditions.

However, if you're skiing here in North America—where they don't make x-c wax yet—then try to figure out which European country's snow conditions approximate the ones you're faced with. Are yours like the snows in Norway, Switzerland, Germany, Finland? If you know this, then lean toward that country's brand or brands in making your selection.

Sounds far-fetched? But sometimes you really can imagine what the snow is like in another country.

Clearing the decks: a glossary

If you're reading about x-c waxing for the first time, it might be a bit confusing to meet terms like "klister," "corn snow," "binder," and such, so let me stop right now and give a few definitions. They'll mean more to you as you read on, but I think they will be easier to refer to if I set them down here, instead of putting them at the end as a sort of summary. And I doubt if it will hurt anybody if the information is repeated later in a different way.

Running waxes: These are the waxes you apply to your ski bottoms and actually ski on.

Binders: Waxes that you apply to your ski for the purpose of holding the running waxes on better; therefore all binders go on before running waxes, and then running waxes cover the binder.

Base waxes: Usually pine-tar compounds, used on wood-bottomed skis to help preserve them.

Hard waxes: Running waxes used primarily for powder snow. These waxes come in small "tins" or small containers. Before application they give the appearance of being "harder" than klisters.

Klister waxes: Running waxes used primarily for granular snow conditions. These waxes come in the tubes, are very sticky, and, if you get things messed up just right, can remind you of an underdone taffy-pull.

Klister snow: Snow that you use klister wax on—almost always snow that has melted and refrozen. There are two categories under this one—frozen granular snow, and corn snow.

Frozen granular snow: Cold, dry, harsh snow that has melted at least once and refrozen. Westerners refer to it as "Eastern Powder Snow."

Corn snow: Granular snow which has started to melt and therefore is wet. It can be just a trifle moist, or quite wet—depending on the temperature.

Cork: A cork used to be a chunk of cork used for smoothing the wax after it's been daubed on the ski. However, nowadays a cork is a cork *or* something synthetic. But at least its use remains the same.

More clearing the decks: color-keyed waxes

Again, you may not want to assimilate all this information right now—but having it here helps to consolidate it for future reference, and

WAX EQUIVALENTS

	Rex	Rode	Swix	Ex-Elit	Holmenkol	Toko	Ostbye	Bratlie
Hard Waxes	Turquoise	———	———	———	———	———	———	———
	Special Green	Special Green	Special Green	Special Kold	Light Green	Olive	Mix	Silke
	Green	Green	Green	Green	Green	Green	Mix	Silke
	Blue	Blue	Blue	Blue	Blue	Blue	Medium	Blandingsfore
	Violet	Violet	Violet	Violet	Violet	Violet	Medium	Blandingsfore
	Red	Red	Red	Red	Red	Red	Mixolin	Klistervoks
	Yellow	Yellow	Yellow	Yellow	Klistervoks	Yellow	Klistervoks	Klistervoks
Klisters	Blue Klister	Blue Klister	Blue Klister	Skar Kristall	Blue Skare	Blue Klister	Skarevoks & Skare	Skarevoks & Green Klister
	Violet Klister	Violet Klister	Violet Klister	Skar Kristall	Red Klister	Violet Klister	Mixolin	Skare
	Red Klister	Red Klister	Red & Yellow Klisters	To Kristall	Yellow Klister	Red Klister	Klister	Vat Klister
	Silver Klister	Silver Klister	———	———	Silver Klister	———	———	———

gives you some terms to fall back on. For the same reason, I'm following it with a Table of Equivalents (color-Keyed under brand names), and a Waxing Chart (showing various waxes for particular temperatures and snow conditions).

To begin with, let me say, in a whisper, that Rex, Rode and Swix waxes are nearly perfectly color-keyed. And, since happily they are the brands most readily available in the United States, I will concentrate on them. If you use another brand, look at the Equivalents table, where you can find the matching waxes of a number of other brands.

I said that Rex, Rode and Swix are *nearly* perfectly color-keyed. There are a few exceptions, though, and I list them below. Except for these, you will know that, say, a Hard Blue—no matter what the brand—will be O.K. for the same snow condition.

1. Rex has a hard wax for very cold powder snow, called Mantyranta or Turquoise. No other brand has an equivalent at this writing.

2. Rex and Rode have a Silver Klister. Swix does not. Silver is

RANGES FOR REX, RODE AND SWIX*

dry snow ——————— increased moisture content ——————> wet snow

Air Temp.	FINE NEW SNOW	OLD POWDER SNOW	GRANULAR SNOW
F.			(crusty or wet corn snow)

Swix Yellow Klister

40 – ....

Red

Red Klister

Rex or Rǿde

35 – ....

Red

Silver Klister

Yellow

32 –

or Purple

Purple Klister

30 – ....

28 – Blue

Blue

25 – ....

Blue

20 – ....

Green

Blue

15 – .... Klister

Green

10 – ....

Special Green

5 – ....

Rex

0 – ....

Turquoise

-5 – ....

dry snow ——————— increased moisture content ——————> wet snow

*where no brand name is given, any may be used.

good for harsh, wet corn snow. It is also a good mixer for use with other klisters, particularly Red and Purple.

3. Swix has a Yellow Klister which is designed for very wet, warm snow. It looks a bit like vaseline. Rex and Rode do not have this wax.

This may seem like quite a few exceptions, but if you compare many other brands (some of which don't even go by the names of colors), you'll find they're more complicated.

The three basic types

All x-c waxes can be divided into three groups: *base* waxes, *binders* and *running* waxes. Let's look at the jobs each does, and see how to apply it to the ski bottoms.

Base waxes

These are mainly pine-tar derivatives that are put on wood bottoms for at least two reasons. First, the pine tar helps seal the bottom. Next, it also helps to hold the running wax you apply on top of it, and pine tar isn't the worst stuff in the world to ski on all by itself. I tar my skis for still another reason: I like the smell of it.

The tars come in instant spray-on, instant wipe-on and just plain old burn-it-in varieties. Usually the spray-ons don't last as long. Some wipe-ons are very good. But if you want to take the time to burn the base into your skis, this is the thing to do.

To prepare your skis for base wax be sure they are clean of any wax or finish that is put on at the factory. Then follow the directions on the can. You should leave the tar fairly dry after you're done.

Note: If you have nonwood bottoms you won't need any pine-tar base; it's only for the wooden skis. I've had kids try to put a base on a plastic bottom, but it sure didn't soak in.

Binders

Binders are used to help hold the running wax on the ski. These days you don't very often need a binder on a wood-bottomed ski, since the running waxes have improved enough so they stay on pretty well, with proper application. I can recall using binder about once during the past three years.

More often, however, it is wise to use binder with a plastic bottom. Situations arise when the snow is harsh, or there is some powder snow mixed in with some icy or granular snow and then the running wax is likely to wear off a hard bottom quite easily. In these cases, the use of a binder will help hold your running wax.

To apply binder, it is easiest to heat the ski, then rub the wax on. If the ski is warm enough the wax will melt on in a thin coat. After the wax is on, go over it again with some heat, and cork it out as smooth as you can get it. The coat you use should be as thin as possible. Binder itself is a very slow wax, and if you get too much on your ski it will *(a)* be difficult to smooth and *(b)* slow you up.

After the binder dries—in a matter of minutes— you are ready to apply the running wax.

Running waxes

Running waxes are the waxes you ski on. The bases and binders hopefully serve their purposes by protecting the ski bottoms and helping to hold on the running wax, but they are not meant to come in contact with the snow.

The running waxes are broken down into two groups: *hard waxes* and *klisters*. The hard waxes usually come in small tins, and the klisters always are packed in what resembles a toothpaste tube.

Here is the cardinal rule for use of running waxes. If you follow this you will be on the right track 99 percent of the time:

ALWAYS USE HARD WAX FOR SNOW THAT IS IN ITS ORIGINAL STATE. USE KLISTERS FOR SNOW THAT HAS MELTED AND REFROZEN.

Thus:

If you are waxing in the middle of a snowstorm, and the snow's melting, use hard wax: the snow has not been refrozen. If you are waxing for some old, very cold snow and the track is very hard, but the snow has never melted since falling, use hard wax.

If the snow has melted, refrozen and is melting again, use klisters. If the snow has melted, refrozen and is very hard, use klisters.

Rather than take a long time to go into specifics like listing each condition and recommending wax for it, I suggest that you study the chart and table on preceding pages. After that, I hope you can make sense out of the manufacturers' directions on the wax containers. (Some of the translations into English aren't so hot: you'll be a lot more enlightened if you can read Finnish, Swedish, Italian, Norwegian or German—even though one company gives the same directions for the use of two of three different klisters!)

In a minute we'll choose a couple of test situations, and work them out with the Waxing Chart.

How to apply wax

Here are a few waxing methods we have adopted during the past few years. They work well for our racers, and they're not too demanding for the family skier.

Using heat

Use of direct heat was *verboten* not so long ago. But I've experimented religiously with heat and can report that I have never ruined a wax job by using a torch. Therefore now, instead of rubbing on hard waxes and then corking in coat after coat, I often heat the ski as described above for applying binder, rub the wax on the ski, heat it again with a torch—and then cork it, or leave it alone.

Corking

Heating the wax with a torch after it is on the ski will do a fairly good job of smoothing it, but if you want to polish it, you should cork it after it has cooled a bit.

Most racers polish their hard waxes with a cork until they glisten. You may notice them some day sighting down the running surface of

33. Using liquid propane fuel to heat skis in a pre-race waxing session.

the ski, looking for the gleam, or for a few rough spots that need more polishing.

Putting on klister

For applying klisters to one pair of skis, the best way is to heat the tube of wax, squeeze it out on to each ski, then heat the ski and smooth out the wax with a paint brush. No muss, no fuss. (We've found that painting with pig-bristle brushes offers the best job. The synthetic-fiber brushes burn easily, and if the burnt bristle ends get stuck in the wax they make a very slow running surface indeed.)

For crowds of skiers, and when I've been in a hurry, I've often punched a few nail holes in the tubes of the chosen klister, thrown them in a pot to melt, and then painted the wax on the skis with a brush. The wax will seep out of a klister tube quite easily—as you know, if you've had the same experience with storage that I have.

Inside—or outside?

Obviously, almost all waxing can be best done in a warm, dry room, with warm skis and warm wax. And I repeat what I stressed years ago: *skis must be bone dry,* or they won't wax right.

There are a few exceptions when it's better to wax outside. A few hard waxes smooth better in the cold. For instance, if you want to use a thin klister base, freeze it, and put hard wax on top of it, you will have the most luck doing this outside, because you're keeping the klister frozen. (Some coaches use a thin klister base instead of a binder. This works well for granular tracks which have some drifted powder here and there. The klister would not do for the powder snow, yet using only hard wax would not do for the granular.)

Klister as a binder

The method of using a thin klister wax as a binder is an example of using wax *thickness* to advantage. The klister, underneath the hard wax, acts as a sort of cushion. In rough, granular snow, the crystals penetrate this cushion and help make the wax work. On smoother snow, the hard wax serves its purpose by being a cushion for these smaller snow crystals *and* acting as a cover for the klister.

Remember, too, that *the thicker the wax, the slower it will be.* Sometimes in race situations you have to compromise between climb and speed. You may have a day when you can't have both to perfection.

Waxing the groove

We usually rub the groove with paraffin wax. Some people prefer to put the regular running wax in the groove, but I would steer clear of doing this.

Often it's the groove area that ices up. If there is a soft running wax in the groove it may pick up more moisture than the regular running surface (since the running surface slides along, in direct contact with the snow, and gets wiped clean during the stride); then, as a result of this moisture, it will ice up. Paraffin will not ice.

Combining waxes

You can, of course, combine any waxes you want to, although there's no guarantee they will work. I have come up with some pretty weird combinations in my memory.

The most common combination is using one wax on the tips and tails and the next softer wax under the foot, for climb. For instance, on

34. The girls are good waxers, can groom their skis with the best.

fairly cold powder snow you might find the best combination is Hard Green on tips and tails and Hard Blue under the foot.

The idea is to use the softer wax under the foot for added climb. Some coaches get even more sophisticated and put a softer wax under the foot on the inside edge of the ski. In climbing, and in most skiing, it's the inside edge of each ski that gets the most use, and this is why they might wax only this part of the ski with a different type.

Another way to combine waxes is to do it the entire length of the ski. Instead of using Green tips and tails and Blue under the foot, you might decide Green was just a bit too hard and Blue just a bit too soft—so you mix them together. I've used this combination with fair success, but it certainly isn't necessary for the average tour. I'm just pointing out different possibilities.

The good waxer is never bound by traditional methods.

Mixing klisters

Klisters are easier to combine than hard waxes because you can just dump them in a little pot, heat them up, and paint them on. This way, you know your exact ratios.

We've used Silver Klister as a mixer quite often, and a word on that would be helpful. Silver seems to be tougher than the softer klisters like Red and Purple (Violet). If there is quite a bit of moisture in the snow or if there is a danger of the klisters wearing, we've found that by adding a bit of Silver—maybe only 1 part in 5, or even less than that—the wax job lasts longer and goes faster.

There are certain situations where one klister will not do the trick. This often happens in the case of Blue. If much of the track is hard frozen granular, yet there are some soft spots—or again, if the snow has quite a bit of moisture in it—the addition of Purple Klister will make a very nice difference.

Variables in waxing

Given the same pair of skis, two people will have different results with the same wax job. One skier might be heavier and therefore need more wax. One might be a better skier and be able to use the same wax more effectively. One might have a technique peculiarly suited for this wax. One might be stronger and more able to make the wax work. One might prefer a certain kind of wax.

Now let's change the skis, and say that two skiers go out with the same wax on their own skis. The situation can still vary. One person might have done a better job waxing. One pair of skis might be more limber, and so the wax will probably hold better. One pair of skis might have more wax on.

Therefore with such variables as these, you can expect that, under the same conditions, different waxes will work for different skiers.

Wax thickness: what it does

If you figure out your conditions and decide to use Hard Green, put it on and go out and find that it slips—then what? The best thing to do is try a thicker coat. The thicker the coat, the better the purchase, or climb. Don't be upset if one coat of wax doesn't do the trick. If you try a couple of coats of Hard Green and it still doesn't work, you had better switch and put some Hard Blue under the foot. Try it.

If conditions are continually changing, though, you may never catch up to the right wax. For a night race in Germany once we went from Hard Green through Blue, Purple, Red and Yellow in the space of 30 minutes. Then our skis still didn't work the way they should have. And no wonder: we had so much wax on them!

Another example. If you are using Bratlie Silke (see the Waxing Chart once more) for cold powder snow, you can vary the thickness of the coat. For very cold snow, a very thin coat is called for. For warmer conditions, put the wax on thicker.

Moisture content in the snow

Lots of times after you have checked the snow and the temperature and the wax tubes or charts, you make your choice and the wax doesn't work at all. Sometimes the moisture content of the snow will change matters.

For instance, if you have a powder snow situation at 15 F. you might try Hard Green—only to find it slips, no matter how much you put on. Blue answers your problem, but according to the chart . . .

If there is a lot of moisture in the snow you will usually need more wax or a softer wax than is normally called for. I've seen situations near zero when we have had to use some Hard Blue.

If you ever see skiers feeling the snow, or trying to make snowballs out of it, they are probably testing for the moisture content. So there are situations when you can't always go by the thermometer. The good waxer will always check the snow. (The Waxing Chart makes note of the moisture content.)

For new snow or hard-packed

All waxes are made so that optimum results are realized when skiing on tracks or hard-packed snow. The difficulties with breaking track, or skiing in powder snow during warm weather, should be clear. If the top surface of the snow is warmish and wet and you push this snow down to mix with colder, drier snow underneath, you have the prime ingredients for icing.

So don't be surprised if a friend tells you he was using a Hard Blue or Purple on his tour while you had to use Yellow. He was probably skiing in new, unbroken snow while you were on a track.

For glazed tracks

It's worth making a few remarks right here about glazed tracks.

When there is a lot of moisture in the snow and in the air, tracks will glaze even at temperatures well below freezing. The snow outside the track remains in a more powdery state. Now you have to make a choice, and that's the way it is with these conditions.

If you want to ski in the track, Klistervoks will work, applied in a thin, thin layer. But step out of the track into the powder and you'll probably ice up.

On the other hand, if you want to ski out of the track you will be sinking into the snow and might even encounter some dry powder beneath the surface. So Hard Purple, or maybe even Blue, would work.

And the weather

It goes without saying that you should have some knowledge of the weather before you go anywhere on skis. Even for a tour, the weather is

---

ABOUT THAT WAX BOX

If you're going to get serious about this waxing, sooner or later you'll need a small box to hold your waxes and equipment. Those boxes for tools or fishing tackle work well. Some skiers use cloth bags; but I don't think these are so convenient, since they're hard to clean, easy to puncture and often wear out.

As a starter you ought to have, in addition to your favorite waxes: a screwdriver and pliers; a couple of corks (hotshots have one cork for very hard waxes and another for not-so-hard waxes— can't mix those waxes on the same cork, you know); a paint brush; spare screws for your bindings and spare screws or nails for your heel plates; steel wool, sandpaper and some rags; a scraper for the ski bottoms and one for the groove, and a file to sharpen the scraper; some wire; adhesive tape or straps for tieing your skis together; matches; hand-cleaner or vaseline; and maybe a wax chart and a thermometer.

important. If you are native to your skiing terrain you will know what is going to happen, regardless of the weatherman's predictions. If you aren't a "local," then you have to depend on the forecast. Use it. It's better than nothing.

Choosing a wax

Let's run a test on a tough waxing situation, trying to interpret the Waxing Chart and Table of Equivalents for what they're worth.

First, determine the snow conditions you'll be skiing in. Then find the appropriate section in the Waxing Chart, and select your wax from one of the three brands—Rex, Rode or Swix. If you use another brand, go to the Table of Equivalents and match the wax from the chart with the wax of the brand you are using. For instance, if your snow conditions call for a Hard Blue and you are using Bratlie wax, you should try the Bratlie Blandingsføre.

Keep in mind that the table is approximate, for a couple of reasons. Some brands, as you see, don't have all the varieties that Rex—Rode—Swix do. And some brands have special waxes designed for conditions not covered so well by R—R—S.

Let's go!

O.K. We'll say you've found the air temperature to be around 29 F., and you have some powder-snow conditions. There is a track you're going to be skiing in; the weather forecast calls for a slight warming trend; it's been fairly warm, in the 20's off and on for a few days, and the snow is old. You squeeze the snow and find there is some moisture in it, or at least it isn't very dry snow.

On the Waxing Chart it may look like a toss-up between a Hard Blue and a Hard Purple. I'd probably start right out with a thin coat of Purple, going on the weather forecast and the fact that the snow is old and moist. If you wanted to, though, you could try a good coat of Hard Blue. If this didn't work, you could then begin to add Purple, perhaps under the foot at first. With an extra layer of Hard Blue on your skis to act as a cushion you might not initially need Purple on the whole length of the ski.

Let's assume that you get enough wax on so it works. Now what?

If you're going to take a tour you'd better throw the next softest wax into your pocket and carry it along for that warming trend. If you got away with using just Blue, take Purple. If you got away with a very thin coat of Purple you might be O.K. with more Purple on your trip, but to be safer you should take another wax. What will it be, Red Hard or that Yellow/Klistervoks? Here again, you will have to make a judgment. If the track is going to warm up and then, through use by skiers, get glazed, you'd better have Yellow along. If the track is going to warm up and stay soft, yet continue to gather more moisture, you will need Red Hard.

Summarizing: The best advice I can think of to tell someone new to x-c waxing is this: First, learn one brand of wax really well before turning to another. Second, watch weather and learn to assess snow conditions. Third, use information supplied by the manufacturer on his wax containers—as far as you can make it out, that is. Fourth, use the Table of Equivalents and the Waxing Chart (and you can always make up your own variations as you progress). Fifth, *remember.* Make a mental note about which waxes you used successfully for which conditions. You don't have to keep a little black book, exactly—though it's not a bad idea for really unusual situations—but you can train yourself to recall problems and solutions from past experience.

And finally, have fun. The heavens aren't going to fall if your wax job wasn't perfect for that family outing.

For the racer: testing waxes

There are many ways to test wax before a race. If you are confident of your waxing ability, the best thing to do is go out and test for yourself and try to avoid being influenced by someone else.

I've seen lots of racers and coaches testing their waxes together. Often they do this on a downhill. The Russians had a system that looked interesting. They put up two poles at intervals along a section of downhill track and timed the skiers as they coasted down it, past the poles. This is O.K.—except for all those variables I mentioned earlier. The fellow with the fastest wax might have had a pair of skis that were slow (i.e., by virtue of their design or stiffness), or he might have been a poor skier and not able to ride his skis as well as the other testers.

Other skiers will coast down a hill and along the flat to see how far they go. Then they compare with another skier who rides the same track. Then they switch skis and make another comparison. Well, this is all right too—but again there are still too many variables for my money. One skier could still ride his skis better than the other; or one might hold a tuck longer, or present less wind resistance.

But this still is not the important point. One wax might be faster at certain speeds than another wax. *At what speed do you want a fast wax?* I maintain that the most important place to have a fast wax is in the initial phase of your forward knee-drive. (We refer to skis that are fast here as being "free.") Try two different waxes as you stride along. Which one is easier to drive ahead? That's the wax to use, even though it might be slower on a downhill section. (If it's slower it won't be far off.) If you consider the number of strides you take during a race and imagine the energy you can conserve by not having to work harder by pushing out a slower ski, then you will have something worth going for.

When I test wax I like to try everything that might work. I never sit at the breakfast table, take out my charts and records, get a weather report and prescribe wax. (The guys that do this ought to be shot.) If there is someone along to help test, all the better. We wax up three to four pairs of skis *with a different wax on each ski,* and go out. It helps to keep secret what is on your skis: then your friend who's testing is more likely to give an honest evaluation of the wax, since some skiers prefer certain brands and would lean toward them, given a choice.

Now, the problem with this method of using different wax on different skis is that you probably use your legs differently. What goes well for the right leg might not work for the left. If you know this, and can compensate accordingly in arriving at a decision, then you're about as close to the ideal as you can get, I believe.

Here's one other consideration.

If the course is full of ups and downs that are fairly steep, and there isn't too much flat terrain, you can use a wax with more climb. It will help you up the steep hills and on the downhills it will break—assuming the downs are fairly steep.

If the course is quite flat, the ups and downs are also flat, so you should use a faster wax. You won't need a lot of climb, and a faster wax really pays off on the flat downhill sections. Often it's the difference between having to pole and not.

Training

The word "training" has many connotations. For some people it represents one of those necessary evils, to others it's a form of gung-ho-ism; some people think of it as being very rugged and a danger to the heart or other parts of the body, and some think it's another form of drudgery.

Of course training should be none of these. I'll give you some of my ideas, and, as before, you can use as many of them as you want.

Training as a way of life

For a long period during my lifetime we Americans have been working hard at improving our lot. This has consisted mainly of getting more material goods, shortening the work week, inventing time-and-labor—saving gadgets and building more vehicles to carry us around—from automobiles to motorcycles and snowmobiles to fancy ride-'em-yourself lawnmowers.

It's no wonder that we seldom posed a threat in the world's premier distance events like the marathon. The rugged, hard living and training necessary to become a champion in the long-distance events had never really been accepted in this country. But now I think the tide is turning. And for several reasons.

Because of our affluence we have lots more leisure time than in former years. People are turning to more and more forms of recreation and a natural outgrowth of this has been an increased interest in all sports. No longer do motorists nearly drive off the road when they see someone out running. It's O.K. now to train, even seriously, because people figure you can do your thing, and they'll do theirs. What the thing is doesn't matter.

35. The U.S. Team on a section of its 800-mile bike trip in August 1970.

These days more people are aware of their physical condition. Many are following some sort of training program prescribed by any one of a number of books on the subject. TV shows frequently have fitness programs. It's becoming one of those "in" things for more people all the time.

As a matter of fact, many tourskiers might be surprised to discover that they're engaging in activities which are considered by most coaches, mind you, as good training.

Take the tourskiers who are hiking because of a love for the woods and mountains and the out-of-doors in general. It's a natural thing for them to be out exercising during the seasons of the year when there is no snow. The lover of hiking doesn't think of himself as training when he's out on a trip in the wilderness. But any coach I know would accept this as training for his athletes.

Naturally, good rugged work around your place—like digging ditches or sawing wood—is good for you.

So no matter what your preference is for various forms of exercise, if you enjoy a certain amount of hard work, if it's part of your lifestyle, then you have it made. You'll be healthier and happier, and you'll have a built-in training program.

Even the serious competitors enjoy hard work and the company of other athletes in their training endeavors. They look forward to long runs or bike rides with their companions and the social aspects combine with the other rewards to make training a way of life.

Train with the same effort you'll ski with

For instance, if you approach tourskiing like walking, and you don't like training *per se,* just forget about "training." Who ever heard of training for walking? Walking is its own training, and you just go about it. Well, you can also do your x-c this way.

If you want to step up a notch and condition yourself for some longer tours of 8 to 10 miles, or if you want to train for a tour race so you can give your rival a good run for his money, then here are several factors you should take into consideration—even if you train only a few times a month.

Training should be varied and enjoyable, challenging, measurable and progressive.

Variety and enjoyment

This is fairly obvious. If your training becomes boring, soon you won't enjoy it. I believe that people who go out and do the same bit of exercise daily have a lot of persistence—more than I have, certainly— and that if they varied their program they would be better off physically as well as mentally.

You don't have to run, run, run all year. You don't have to bike, hike, jog or lift weights continuously either.

Vary it. If whatever you're doing begins to get dull, or isn't fun any more, *change something.* Do something different, go out with different people, take some time off. Don't be afraid to have some fun in your training. Almost anything goes as long as it's good exercise.

36. We did enjoy it—honest. Just 200 yards before setting a new record for 270 miles of the Long Trail (9 days, 4 hours) in 1969.

The challenge

If your training has a bit of a challenge to it, you'll ultimately feel the rewards for having done it. I don't think it's much to go out and do something that's real easy and doesn't make me puff more than once or twice. My chest swells right up, though, after I've accomplished a decent sort of workout.

The challenge can take many forms. There may be a particular goal you have in mind, like running a hill on your route without stopping to walk, or biking a certain section of road in a given time, or hiking over a mountain range in so many hours. Or you might have a standard piece of work to complete in a given time. And the challenges can vary. What's right for you may be too tough or too easy for the next guy.

The measurement

You can measure your progress or ability to do a workout in many different ways. The most common method is to time yourself for the duration of a specific workout. You might occasionally run a course for time, and see how your new time compares with earlier ones.

But you can also measure yourself by how you feel. I think this is the most important measurement. Unless you're vying for the Olympic track team, no one expects you to run a sub-four-minute mile, so if you happen to be running a mile for training it's not important to time yourself. See how you feel after it's done. If you're limber, relaxed and exhilirated, what more can you ask?

However, if you want to begin checking your progress because you're on a special program, with goals in mind, then you will probably want to time yourself once in a while. But try to steer away from the stop-watch if you're training solely for skiing.

Progress

Your training should show some progress.

Now, I don't mean that you have to gain and gain, say, in running a loop of a couple of miles. If you're a young whippersnapper I would expect progress in terms of shortened times required to run given distances. But if you're middle-aged and you hold your ground in doing certain workouts—boy, that's progress too! Every once in a while when I get discouraged about my training I compare myself with other people my age and then I don't feel bad at all.

By all means, *don't set your sights too high too soon.* Make your progress slowly. Chip away at it and take your time. If your goals are attainable you'll get an extra psychological boost. Too many people go on crash programs and try to improve too fast, only to suffer setbacks, get discouraged and quit.

That built-in control

Fortunately, when most people exercise too hard they don't feel on top of the world, exactly, and so they slow down. If you are training you should at least use that feeling of discomfort as a warning signal. If you experience pain anywhere, slow down or stop whatever you're doing. Rest for a day or two, or more; and next time out try something less rugged.

I've been told that some young people with strong hearts can work or exercise themselves to the point of exhaustion, or until some part of the body stops functioning properly—like legs not responding to efforts to make them move—and not do themselves any harm in this process. I've never seen a situation like this and really don't want to. I don't think that you, either, should expect your legs, say, to stop moving when you are near the point of overtaxing yourself.

In fact, if you are in your middle years you ought to have a check-up from your doctor before you embark on any sort of training program: if you're a student or younger, you should be under the supervision of a coach. Therefore *I'll assume that you have had a medical examination by your family doctor or your school doctor.*

The cardiovascular system

Most of the training for distance events like x-c races is concentrated on improving the cardiovascular system—that is, developing an athlete's ability to pump or deliver oxygen-carrying blood to all parts of the body. There is a great deal of debate over the most efficient way to train your system, and if you read enough of the literature you can find almost any theory you like. But there's one thing for sure: not many doctors, at least in this country, have studied very much about training for x-c skiing. There are lots of articles written about distance events in track, but few on skiing.

Skiing as a distance event is so relatively new in this country that few physiologists have focused on it. Because of the lack of information on x-c training many coaches err in relating training for skiing with training for the running events in track. In x-c skiing, though, the upper-body muscles of the back, shoulders and arms come into play much more than they do in straight foot-running. Many believe that the slight upper-body build is an advantage for track; on the other hand, if you didn't have enough strength in your upper body for x-c you'd be finished.

Then too, running an x-c ski race is a series of extremely high-effort periods interspersed with other periods of rest when you go downhill. The rest in running on a circular track doesn't come until the race is over. And even the rest a cross-country footracer gets on downhill sections isn't all peaches and cream.

With the Winter Olympic Games scheduled for Colorado in 1976 you can be sure that more medical attention will be given to training for the ski events. Doctors around the country are already beginning to work on this.

Training roundup for tourskiers

I'd like to list the different training workouts that the members of the U.S. Team do, but first let me finish summarizing my theories on your training (assuming you aren't headed for the Olympics in '76).

1. If engaging in activities considered "training" is a way of life for you, you will be in good shape and will never have to worry about a "formal" training program.

2. All-round body strength is necessary for x-c skiing. The best way to condition yourself for x-c skiing is to ski cross-country. That should be obvious. But during the off-season if you are thinking about your training, do something for your legs, arms, shoulders and back. You'll find specific ski-oriented exercises described in a minute.

37. "Putney armbands"–bicycle inner-tubes–for poling exercise.

3. The best-conditioned people in the world are the ones who have a good cardiovascular system. Bulging muscles are not an indication of this. You can't discount the fellow who is carrying around something that looks like a beer belly either. Dr. Kenneth H. Cooper's books on Aerobics treat this subject quite well.

U.S. Team training components

Members of the U.S. National Team group their training in five different categories. A well-rounded program contains workouts from each category almost every week during the year. Many of the athletes train twice a day, five to six days a week during the year. This is the extreme in dedication. You have the Olympics in mind when you train like this.

I'll list each category and make a few comments, giving examples.

Endurance or distance

This is just what it says: a long workout that's designed to build endurance in the athlete. *A rough guide for the time of the workout is twice the time it takes to race the event you're training for.* Therefore some of the boys training for the 50-km race—which takes around 3 hours—go out for as long as 6 hours at a clip.

Many physiologists, coaches and trainers feel that distance training is the most important aspect of any athlete's program.

Running, jogging, biking, hiking in rugged terrain or with a pack, canoeing, kayaking, rather heavy work like logging or pick-and-shovel jobs—all qualify as methods of endurance training. Another rough guide is this: *Your heartbeat should average right around 120 per minute, counting spurts and lags, during these workouts.*

Interval training

Interval training is repeated exercises broken up by "rest" periods.

The most common type of interval training is running. Athletes run a prescribed distance at a fixed speed, return to the start and rest, or jog a bit until they are rested, and run again. There are lots of variables here—the number of intervals you do, the distance you run, the speed with which you run, and the amount of time you rest. For instance, the number of repetitions might vary from 5 to 50, the distance from 50 yards to several hundred yards, the speed at which you run from half-effort to all-out, and the rest from partial to fairly complete.

Here are a couple of rough guides to help you with your interval training.

Rest after each set until your heart rate goes down to 120 per minute (I'm assuming you worked hard enough to get it up over 120). Get a rough approximation of the recovery time you need to get your pulse back down. Continue with the exercises until your recovery time is quite a bit longer than it was at first, or until you feel tired doing your workout. If doing an interval workout seems to take too long—i.e., that it takes too long to get tired or to slow down your recovery rate—then you can work harder or longer at your particular exercise. For instance, you might be running 60-yard intervals and find it takes a

38. An early-season drill: matching stride for stride on parallel tracks to compare styles, strength and tempo.

long time to get the effect of having had a workout. So jump the distance to 80 or 100 yards and run faster.

One theory behind interval training is that while you are waiting for your heart rate to return to 120 you are actually conditioning your cardiovascular system because of the stress it is under. Herein lies the beauty of interval training. During a period of 20 minutes of interval training, you might actually be resting or jogging, *while your recovery takes place,* for 12 to 14 minutes. In other words, your leg muscles, etc., are not being called upon to perform under stress for more than 6 to 8 minutes.

Proponents of the interval-training method claim that in addition to being a good conditioner for the cardiovascular system, it at the same time improves your ability to recover from vigorous exercise.

You can do lots of things for interval training. The more common approaches are running, biking, swimming or rowing rather vigorously for short periods of time. But, during a distance workout, you could incorporate some interval training by going fast for a stretch and then taking it easy (like jogging while running, coasting while biking or skiing, etc.) for a while until your recovery was complete.

Speed/tempo training

This kind of training is interpreted two ways. Generally, tempo training means training at racing speed, for whatever event you are working for. Speed training can mean this also; but it is used by some to mean sprint, or top-speed, training. I shall use it as meaning sprinting or going all-out.

Generally, all the exercises you use for interval training will qualify for tempo and speed training.

Tempo training

Tempo training is used to condition yourself for performing at racing speeds. It is so similar to interval training that often the two kinds of workouts are lumped together. Sometimes tempo training takes place for periods of time equal to 1/3 to 2/3 of the time required to run the event you're training for.

Speed training

Speed training is used to train the body to be able to perform faster. I've already said something about high tempo training in the Technique chapter. With speed training, by my definition, you go all-out for a rather short period of time, then take a good rest by waiting until the pulse is well under 120 per minute, and repeat.

Strength training

This is done to make yourself stronger. There are lots of good weight-lifting programs, but if you are going in to one of them, be sure you have the advice of someone competent in this area. There's no sense straining or injuring yourself through ignorance.

I count three kinds of physical strength. One is gained by weight-lifting, which is especially good for those muscles involved in lifting weights—and these are not always the same ones that you need in skiing.

Another kind of strength is gained by doing special exercises related

39. Martha Rockwell of the U.S. Women's Team leads other girls in hill-running with poles. A good ski-oriented exercise.

to the skiing motions, like pulling on tough elastic ropes ("Putney armbands" for this exercise are shown in Photo 37).

The third kind of strength training is that which develops what I call over-all, coordinated body strength. When you get out there skiing you have to put it all together. The fellow who can press a lot of weight or pull the armbands until the cows come home is not necessarily going to be able to combine all his movements into a strong, coordinated effort on the ski track. Certain kinds of exercises like rock-climbing and gymnastics are very good for this coordinated strength.

Other hard work like shoveling, digging ditches (without a backhoe), cutting wood with an axe, chain-saw (these are O.K.), or cross-cut, all qualify. Hiking with heavy packs is good.

Coordination and ski-oriented exercises

Cross-country skiing and badminton are two of the most underrated sports in this country as far as physical demands are concerned. If you

40. Roller skiing in early November as a tuner-upper for skiing muscles.

think there's nothing to badminton, get out there on the court with a pro some day. Likewise, if you think x-c can't be a real workout, just jump in the track behind a member of the U.S. Team and see how you fare. (A friend who didn't know any better told me once that all there was to x-c skiing was "getting your wind and a little bit of a stride." I almost jumped down his throat.)

I feel that any training you can do in other sports, and especially any coaching you can get in other sports during the off-season, is going to help you with your coordination and therefore help you with your x-c technique. These are all good: playing different games like softball, soccer, tennis, or doing tumbling and trampoline work, or diving. We've even had instruction in modern dance for members of the U.S. Team, and it was well received.

A recent trend in ski training has been toward any ski-oriented exercise you can perform off snow. These include hill-running with poles, roller skiing (as in Photos 39 and 40), and use of armbands to simulate the poling motions, mentioned earlier. There is no doubt that these exercises will help your conditioning and your technique.

Remember, if all other factors like training, strength, wax, etc., are equal, the skier with the best technique is going to win the race.

Summarizing: The best training programs contain a balance of all these different components. It is no dice to short-cut one or two phases. And don't think that if you practice learning good technique to make up for lack of training, you'll make it. In a big race with stiff competition you'll get so tired from lack of conditioning that you won't be able to use your technique.

Ideas for team training on snow

Often you can combine some ski training with some technique work. For instance, as you do certain kinds of interval training you can also practice flat or uphill technique. So most of the exercises listed below will help your technique as well as improving your conditioning.

On the flats

1. Follow a good skier, stride for stride, so that only a foot or so separates the rear of his ski and the front of yours. This way you can see the power of his stride and get a good workout as you do it.

2. Make parallel tracks and ski beside another person. If you are a coach this is a good way to observe where the faults and excellences are. As a skier, you can also get a good feel for how the other fellow is doing.

3. Follow-the-leader is always fun, especially if you switch the lead often. Hard-packed or granular snow is usually most suitable for this.

4. We've spent lots of time mimicking other skiers, especially well-known international ones. This is a form of technique training in that you try for a special effect or style in your skiing by copying someone.

We've had fun imitating the general styles of the Scandinavians. Several Norwegians ski with a straightforward, classic style, and these skiers are good to copy. But then there are the others who have quirks like the Swedes, who often ski very vigorously, but not too smoothly. Many Finns copy Mantyranta, who had a very distinctive arm-carry, particularly when he was shifting gears, or going from a single-pole to a double-pole. The favorite of all, however, is Walter Demel, the German. He "agitates" around the track so much that we call him "The Human Bendix." Washing machine or not, he sure wins his share of races.

Up hills

Since about half the time during a race is spent skiing up hills, it's a good idea to spend about half the Team's time on uphill training. Anyone can practice the different techniques very easily if he has a hill that is fairly flat at first, then gets gradually steeper until he's forced to resort to a herringbone to get to the top.

Shifting gears

Coaches can stand on the side of the hill and observe how well their skiers handle each situation—flat-skiing technique on the gradual uphill, hill-running on the steeper section, and the herringbone on the steepest section. Some skiers will shift gears earlier than others.

In addition, it's always interesting to time the skiers as they use different techniques, and then determine the fastest method of getting up a hill.

Effort after the climb

Lots of skiers die out once they reach the top of a hill. After some practice it's worth taking your hill course across the top and perhaps another hundred yards, or at least to the next downhill section. Two skiers might have the same time up a hill, but one could gain several seconds on the other because of a continued effort at the top.

Down hills

1. Find a downhill section with a straight outrun and take turns coasting down it. The person who can coast out the farthest has

the best downhill crouch and/or the best wax. You'll be surprised at the differences here.

2. Set up easy slalom courses and race them. Or set up slalom courses on the flat and race them. This is good double-poling practice.

3. Find a good downhill section, open, and have freestyle championships to see who comes down with the most elan. Powder-snow conditions are ideal for this. You'll need an impartial judge, what with all the hoopla.

A few poling exercises

1. Double-pole across a flat section, or a slight incline, up or down, *using no strides: keep skis together.*

2. Double-pole using just one step for each poling action. Use the same foot for a while, then shift and use the other foot; continue, alternating the lead foot.

3. Single-pole across a flat using no steps or strides.

4. Single-pole, up a slight hill, again using no strides.

After the workout

After some good exercise the best thing you can do is come in and take a shower, hot bath or a sauna. Then, cool off gradually and rest awhile.

Many young racers come in after a competition, change their clothes and "go dancing." Well, even the young bodies need some time to recuperate. If you don't take care of yourself you will wear down and make yourself more susceptible to colds and minor injuries like muscle strain.

I noticed the top Russian athletes in 1970 all taking long rests of several hours after their distance events. They feel this is the best way for the body to recover to a normal state.

Lots of skiers wonder what to drink after sweating profusely. The current thinking espouses the importance of replacing body liquids, even during races—hence the food stations in 30- and 50-km events. For many years coaches felt a high concentration of sugar or dextrose was good to feed during and after racing or heavy exercise, but now the emphasis is on the quantity of liquid instead of the strength. You should replace what you lose through perspiration.

The popular drinks like Sportade and Gatorade are not loaded with energy, but rather have minerals like salt in them which replace those body minerals lost through sweating. It may sound crazy to you that an athlete would gulp down a salt-flavored drink during a race, but we do it and it seems to work fine.

Diet

During the days before a race, or any rugged exercise, all the athletes I've encountered stay on a regular diet.

Then as the race day approaches many will begin to concentrate more on carbohydrates, or at least they'll cut down on fatty foods. The thinking here is that by eating plenty of carbohydrates the body will store up all the blood sugar it can, to be used during the race. Also, on race days carbohydrates are more easily digested and converted to energy.

But, here again you can find all sorts of different approaches. Our friends the Russians had roast chicken every morning before their races in Czechoslovakia. I've heard lots of athletes and coaches say you shouldn't eat anything during the three hours preceding a race and what you eat before then should be rather light at that. Well, chicken an hour and a half before a race doesn't qualify for that theory. I'll take the Russians' results, though, and their diet!

Family fun

When our kids were younger we used to take the whole tribe—four of them—out on x-c jaunts. Skiing began, literally, right in our back yard, and it was easy to get waxed up and go for short hikes.

By the time the youngest was five we felt we could really cover the ground and then took longer trips. The older boys would ski ahead, breaking trail or making tracks for us. If a couple of the family got too far ahead and had to wait for the slower skiers, or for a birdwatcher, they'd practice short downhill sections, or sneak around behind to surprise the rest of the group.

To help encourage our kids, especially when they were three or four years old, we used to plan predominantly downhill routes, with a car waiting at the other end. What a welcome sight it was for a youngster after a 3-mile trip!

Follow-the-leader was, and still is, one of our favorite things. A few years ago it was easy for my wife and me to follow the twists and turns of the leader. But now, if one of the boys is leading the pack, we have to watch out or we'll end up in a brook or the middle of a pine tree.

We've practiced tucks on long downhill sections, Telemark turns, jumps, jump turns, "queersprungs" and fence-jumping.

We've played some form of Fox-and-Geese, or Ski Chase. Give one skier, or a couple of them, a head start and let them ski off, leaving trail markers occasionally. The object is to track them down. If there is new snow it will take a clever fellow to keep from being caught quite soon. He can double back eventually and get into the tracks of those chasing him; then there's bound to be a little confusion.

Picnic stuff

On our lunch trips we always made sure that each skier had one light wrap-around shirt or jacket extra. This provided enough warmth for

41. Fooling around, waiting for the last few to show up . . .

sitting and eating our snacks. Our fare usually consisted of Triscuits and peanuts; candy such as chocolate; cheese; raisins, apricots, dates or other dried fruit; and oranges. I could fit this all in a fanny pack or a loose, frameless backpack. (A frame pack tends to get in the way of my poling.) It wasn't much trouble to carry the pack, especially after lunch!

Our kids got a big kick out of making a small fire to stand around during lunch. There were always plenty of dead branches on the lower parts of the trees. Getting these provided a few interesting situations. Often the snow has melted, or is hollowed out near the base of a tree, and more than once we temporarily lost one of the smaller kids in that pit around the tree.

If you're a camera bug, by all means take some pictures of your little trips. You'll get more kicks out of viewing the pictures as the years go by.

We were always familiar with our territory and stayed fairly close to home, or near a road where we could go in the event of a broken ski or something like that, so I didn't take any extra equipment along.

For longer jaunts

However, if I was going out for an extended trip with a larger group, in new terrain, I'd take the following as a minimum:

A spare, plastic ski tip
A cake of paraffin and the next softest ski wax we might need
Combination knife/screwdriver
Small roll of adhesive tape
Matches

Taking overnight trips, complete with sleeping bags, tents, cooking utensils, etc., is another matter which I am not going to cover. I like camping, but in the winter I prefer to put most of my energy into skiing. However, Hurley and Osgood have written a nice book on this subject of winter camping and I refer you to it.

Ideas for other trips

If you're part of a larger group which includes two cars, take a cross-over trip. Park the cars at opposite ends of your route, have each group meet in the middle of the tour for lunch, and proceed. Don't forget to exchange car keys at lunch.

Get hold of some pamphlets on ski-orienteering and set up a course for that. This is a very popular sport in Scandinavia which combines map-reading and skiing skills. It's a good way to learn to read maps; and you'll need compasses for this.

You can get maps of new territory and explore it, without compasses. This is fun and it's O.K. as long as it isn't snowing so as to wipe out your ski tracks. I'd hate to get lost and not have tracks to follow back to my starting point.

Night skiing

Night skiing on lighted tracks is gaining here in North America and, if you get a chance, you should try it. Better yet, try to get a group together to build your own little loop, string up some carnival lights, use street lights, automobile headlights, bonfires, torches, or anything that will provide some illumination.

Once or twice a year, when there is a little powder snow on top of a good base, and the moon is full, we go out night skiing. This is some thrill!

42. Off with friends on a tour in new spring powder snow.

You know those bright nights when you can see your shadow on the snow? Try it. It's quite good for your balance, since you can't see all the very small ripples in the track and you have to learn to relax and absorb the little bumps.

Finally, if you don't have a lighted track, and the moon isn't just right for you, get a headlamp and go out on your own. These are coming on the market now and are very handy. The lamp is light, attaches to your head with a headband, and is powered by a battery pack which you carry on your belt.

Here's one situation where you'll want to avoid a lot of bobbing of the head, or bouncing around looking from side to side. If you want to see where you're going you'll have to keep the lamp pointed directly ahead.

Organizing
a tour race

This chapter is primarily for people who organize races of any sort, from small club affairs to the large tour races that are cropping up all over North America.

If you are thinking of entering a tour race some day you might be interested in reading this to see what goes on behind the scenes, so to speak, in getting these races organized. You should also see the listing of races in the Where It's At chapter.

In a few years I think there will be upwards of 50,000 competitors entering tour races annually. Why the sudden interest?

Clearly, there are an increasing number of tourskiers every year. And lots of them get a charge out of pitting themselves against friendly rivals, or against younger, stronger competitors. They enjoy the group atmosphere, the notable camaraderie of these get-togethers. After all, in what other sport can you find six-year-olds, housewives, middle-aged businessmen, grandparents and Olympic athletes in the same field, running against each other?

Most of our well-established tour races had informal beginnings. I recall the first Washington's Birthday Race in 1963—the prototype for such events—when Eric Barradale gathered a group of us on the slopes of Hogback Mountain Ski Area in southern Vermont and set us hurtling down toward Brattleboro. Eric hopped in his car and drove to the finish to time us and extend greetings. It was almost a one-man show. But now this race is the subject of several meetings per year, and committees abound, doing their jobs in the organization.

I'll go into some detail in describing the functions of different committees that might be necessary for running a race with a field of 1,000 or more. Naturally, for smaller races you can combine work assignments.

And don't worry about eclipsing those one-man shows. They'll continue. Many a skier prefers their informality.

43. The height of neighborliness: starting a race in your front yard.

The organizers

O.K. Some people decide to stick their necks out and run a race. They are *it!* Their job is to round up as many volunteer committees as possible and assign them duties. In addition, they usually decide on such matters as the course, the field, entry fees, and who handles the paper work and phone calls. There are no definite rules for running these races. But if you want to refer to organization tables used for running official U.S. Ski Association events, you might get some clues. These tables are necessary for only the important sanctioned races like National and divisional championships, Olympic tryouts, etc.

> *Note:* Most of the work in successful races is done in advance—laying out a good trail, preparing a good track, getting race entries and information in, and lining up plenty of help. One of the most discouraging events is a race run by a few well-meaning officials who get overburdened with

work and simply can't do everything well and/or promptly. They deserve a lot of credit, and certainly thanks, for their devotion to x-c. Therefore it's doubly sad to see any ball-up at race time which could have been avoided by nailing details down better beforehand.

The course

Some races use a loop, or trail, that begins and ends in the same place. This is like most cross-country ski races.

Some races are run from one location to another. I prefer this kind, even if only for the psychological reason of going somewhere. It's nice to be able to say, for instance, that I toured from Westminister West to Putney.

Many tour races use the same trail every year. This way, skiers can compare times from one year to another, and even though snow conditions are faster some years than others, it makes for an interesting addition to the race.

The length of the courses varies from a few kilometers to the real long ones—like Sweden's Vasa, which is 85 km. A standard which is popular on this continent is between 10 and 15 km. However, if you have a nifty course in mind which might go longer you shouldn't worry about it too much. Advertise the length and any tourskiers who thinks it's a bit too long should take it easy, or not enter the race. Even a course of 20 km shouldn't give the practiced tourskier much trouble if he paces himself.

The field

Most of the races have been open to anyone who can ski x-c over the course. I can foresee the time when some races get so crowded that they will have to be limited by age, sex, or just first-come-first-served. But right now, most entrants in the bigger races get a chance to compare their times with former Olympian and National Team members. At the 1971 Washington's Birthday Tour in Putney, the first six finishers were members of the U.S. National Team. That's O.K. Lots of people get a kick out of saying, "I raced against So-and-so, and finished just fifteen minutes behind him. He probably had better wax. And of course he's been training. Etc."

Entry fees

We used to run our races for $1.00 per person. With inflation, added demands and complications involved in organization, those days are gone. I think it's a fair assumption that the racers should pay enough entry money to take care of any of the following expenses: printing entry blanks; secretarial help; stationery and postage necessary for sending out information, press releases, entry blanks and results; racing bibs; simple refreshments for the skiers (described later); insurance; professional help hired, such as snowplowing, policing road-crossings and parking; use of parking lots; certain maintenance work that has to be done on the trail.

I'll discuss prizes and souvenirs for finishers in a moment.

Paper work and phone calls

If you want to be barraged with letters and phone calls before a big race, just offer your name and phone number as part of the mailing address on the entry form. You'll get personal requests of every sort, and your phone won't stop ringing until days after the race is over.

Every growing race organization reaches a point where certain things have to be made impersonal for the sake of efficiency. For instance, have your entries sent to Race Secretary, c/o some business, school, or club address, or to a post-office box rented for the purpose (annual rent is nominal, and certainly worth the saving in peace of mind alone).

The trail committee

The trail location should be determined during the off season, well before snowtime. It should be cut and cleared—and measured (everyone wants to know how far he skied). It is particularly important to avoid steep downhills, and all downhill sections should be followed by a straight, flat outrun. If the trail is out of the wind and if there aren't too many sections facing the south sun you'll have fewer maintenance problems.

Ideally, the loop type of trail should be 1/3 uphill, 1/3 level and 1/3

44. *The result of all that work on trail and track.*

downhill. If you are going from one location to another, though, you'll probably attract more skiers if you use a downhill route—i.e., if there's an altitude difference between the start and finish points, choose the lower ground for the finish.

First: manners

After you've got the course in mind, you do what is the most important thing of all: *call in person on landowners and get their permission for the race to cross their property.* You should have insurance, and therefore be able to assure each landowner that he is not liable for damages in case of a mishap. If he wants his land used *only* for the period of the race, this fact must be made clear later on to all entrants (some of whom might otherwise want to train the course beforehand). Of course any cutting, leveling or clearing to make a good trail must also be O.K.'d in advance.

In return, remember that it never hurts to repair fences or cut up some fireplace wood for people whose land you use. Finally, after the race is over, don't forget formal thanks.

With tools in hand . . .

Some shoveling or bulldozing may be necessary to smooth the trail. Sidehill sections where one ski is lower than the other are to be avoided, both from a skier's and a track-setter's standpoint.

On certain stretches you should think of how snow will weigh down tree branches hanging over the heads of skiers who are on a trail a couple of feet deep in snow. Then you'll realize that clearing limbs and brush to a height of 6 or 7 feet isn't enough. Get the tall guys in the trail-clearing group to do the high work.

After all this is done, and if you have any time left, it's really fine to place markers every kilometer or mile along the trail, and to make a detailed map of the course.

Race secretaries and duties

I'm using this group as my catch-all. You'll see why when you read further. There are lots of odd jobs that can be done and, while some of them might logically fall under another special committee's function, I've just chosen to put them here for emphasis.

There are the ordinary duties of getting out entry blanks, arranging for whatever prizes are decided on, accepting entries, making up the running order or assigning bib numbers, handing out numbers on the race day (and collecting them if this is necessary), keeping times and scoring results, typing up results and mailing them out—and this is just a start. Some of the secretaries will need executive ability, or should be members from the organizing committee.

Entry blanks

How elaborate your entry form is—whether it's mimeographed or printed, and how much information it carries beyond the bare facts and regulations—depends on your budget and manpower, but here are a few ideas which I've seen used over the years.

Timing. If the blanks are mailed out too far in advance, the human tendency is to set them aside for future decision and maybe forget them altogether. If mailed too close to race time, either they come too late for many would-be entrants to make it, or the secretary is drowned in a flood of last-minute paper work. A good compromise: *mail them three weeks before the race.*

Information on the blank. Necessary are: race committee's mailing address; date, starting place, length of race; entry fee (and when/how to send it), classes; and stipulations concerning early and late entries, eligibility and refunds; names of cooperating organizations or co-sponsors.

A simple map of the trail, with a profile of the course (flats, ups, downs) is almost a must. This can indicate distance and direction from nearest major highways, and locate parking and viewing areas.

Also important to mention are availability of toilets, food, waxing facilities; method of start (mass or interval); if there are shuttle buses from parking to start (if they're needed), plus any additional amenities which may be provided by the time the race starts.

Remember that the more details you can include on the blank, which the entrant can keep for reference, the more you'll be saved from having to answer questions on the morning of the race. It says here.

Racing bibs

We've gone to using paper racing bibs, handing them out the day of the race and letting the competitors keep them as a momento. At this writing, they cost only about 35 cents, and we include that in the entry fee. This saves the time and labor involved in collecting cloth numbers at the end of the race. A set of several hundred cloth numbers presents a real management problem when they're dirty, wet, and several are missing from the order.

Publishing results

We try to get our results out as soon as possible. If the recorders have cards with all the racer information on them (prepared in advance as entries were processed, and used as described after Timing), and then file them according to finish order, you can have a typist start on a stencil while the race is in progress—*if it's a mass-start affair.*

During the last Washington's Birthday Race at Putney we were able to get out sheets of results as the race progressed. Shortly after the last finishers came in we had the complete results out. It doesn't take any more time to do it this way, during the race, than it does after the race.

Racers really appreciate having results published soon after they finish. They are high with excitement and want to see how they have done. To wait around a few hours, or go home and wait for mail results, takes a lot from the day.

Prizes and awards

We've never made a big deal out of prizes, sensing that the tourskier's reward comes from doing the race rather than collecting a doodad to display in his corner cupboard. U.S. Team members who have run in our southern Vermont tour feel the same way, enjoying the carefree competition.

Since the first Washington's Birthday race here in 1963, the name of each year's over-all winner has been engraved on a permanent trophy donated by a local jeweler; the token piece of silverplate for the winner to keep was also given by friends of x-c, not bought from race funds.

Always, though, the emphasis was on an inexpensive small memento to be given each finisher—nowadays it's a special little certificate mailed out after the race, officially acknowledging the skier's participation and official time. In addition, there have been modest prizes—again donated, and chosen to be useful—for class winners. These have been such things as wax, wax remover, corks, gadgets like that. A good deal of fun in planning a race is figuring out ways to acknowledge the special contribution to the sport made by nonwinners. Therefore it's nice to have a little prize for the oldest competitor and the youngest, or for the one who traveled farthest to get to the race, or the family with the most entrants, etc.

Group scoring

In some of the tour races in Scandinavia they use a scoring system for clubs. This can be as simple as track scoring and adds a little incentive for the groups who take part. Simply score, say, the first ten finishing places from each club. Add them up, and the low-total group wins a rotating trophy; or, the high-score club provides the refreshments at the next get-together.

Arranging for wax information

If you can find a coach or some veteran racers who are willing to

45. *Kids checking out veteran Bob Gray's waxing ideas before a race.*

stick their necks out and prescribe wax for the competitors, it makes for a nice gesture. Lots of tourskiers admit to being in the dark about waxing and are grateful for any advice they can get.

If there are elevation changes in your course, and you want to be really flossy, you can post air temperatures, as recorded along the course, for help with waxing prior to the race. This would be most helpful for those who are waxing on their own, possibly disregarding any official waxing information given by someone in the know.

Track preparation

The best way to prepare tracks for x-c skiing is by using a snowmobile or some snow-compacting machine and a track sled. (Photo 46).

Ideally, the swath you pack should be 5 to 6 feet wide and the tracks should be set in from 2 to 4 inches deep and from 6 to 8 inches between the inside edge of each ski. If you are expecting lots of skiers and have the space, make double tracks—two sets, parallel—on your trail.

At Putney we have two snowmobiles, a big one and a small one, which we use rather effectively. For practice sessions, one pass with the big machine and the sled is good enough. For races we go over the trail two or three times to get some of that extra width.

Using the trail equipment

There are several hints I can give which should be helpful. In our area we have had lots of experience with snow-packing and have learned many things the hard way. The comments I make will be appropriate for machines like our snowmobiles—SkiDoos, Olympique and Alpine—and our track sled. If you have a snowcat, then you're in a different league: you can use a much bigger sled and do a better job.

First of all, be careful. Running a snowmobile can be exhausting work. Getting stuck out there in the boondocks and having to lift the machine out of deep snow, or holes, or from in between trees, is rugged. Be sure to take along a shovel and an axe whenever you go far from any roads.

Level trails. If your trail is level, it will make for easier snowmobiling. The machines aren't too effective crossways on sidehills, even when you lean out and make like an outrigger to keep them going straight up or down. In fact, if you have a lot of sidehill terrain you are in for a few thrills. During the summer we chip away at our sidehills with shovels or bulldozers, gouging skiable shelves across the faces of the hills.

Watch out for dips in the trail. It's those small ones that get you: the runners on the machine are headed uphill, the tail end is headed downhill, and the drive belt is suspended, spinning madly. Fill the dips in. They might be ski-breakers anyway.

Pack the trail after every snowfall of six inches or so. If you wait until you have a depth of two feet of unpacked snow it will be very difficult to pack the trail, particularly the uphill sections. Most of the snowmobiles don't lack for power, as you may know, but they do need traction.

Working on uphills. There are a couple of methods we use for our uphills. If the snow is deep even after one storm, we take both vehicles out and play leapfrog. One goes uphill as far as it can without getting stuck, peels off and returns to the foot. The other vehicle follows the first's tracks and can get up farther before peeling off and coming back.

Another system is to run the course so that you can take the steep uphills going downhill, by going backwards on the course. Usually, if you machine down a hill you can turn around and come back up it. If the hill is so steep you can't do this, it's probably too steep for the course.

If you can't run the course backwards, or take the hills the way you would like to, it often helps to foot-pack up the hill before trying it with the machine. One trip up and back will usually do the trick.

You should never pack a trail during warm weather if you know freezing weather will follow soon. If you pack it and draw the moisture up through the snow, or actually compress the snow and the moisture, when it freezes you'll have an ice rink and unpleasant x-c conditions.

When to put in the track

When you pack a trail be sure not to let it set up, or freeze, too long before putting in the track. The best system is to drag the track sled right behind the machine, and pack and set the track at the same time. This may not be possible because of the snow depth or the terrain. If it isn't, do a small section of packing, then set the track. If you wait until the next day, the packed snow may be too hard. This is especially apt to happen if there is a lot of moisture in the snow.

If you have to go around a few times before setting the track, leave for the last trip the middle section where you intend to set track. Then attach the sled and set the track.

If your machine is powerful enough and the conditions are right, you can drag a skier on a towrope behind the track sled. This gives you the perfect system. It is important to ski in the tracks set by the sled soon after they're made. The tracks freeze and, if they are not skied in, ski bindings will catch on the sides when the first skiers use the tracks later on.

If you have the track set and it warms up, it's best to keep the skiers off.

If this is not possible, then here's a neat trick that will save your track. Just as the weather starts to cool, or after the skiers are done with the track, go around it with the snowmobile and a big, heavy chain

46. *The bottom of a track sled that's set over 1,000 miles of x-c tracks (7 inches between inside edges of runners—a good width for racing).*

looped behind the snowmobile. The chain will wipe out the old track, or fill it in, and leave your trail looking like a new carpet. After the weather freezes you will have a loose granular condition instead of two icy ruts. Then weight the track sled and go around it again.

> *Note:* Posting the trail before the race is a good idea. This could keep someone from ruining your tracks with a snowmobile, or even with a pair of snowshoes.

Setting tracks in ice

In very icy conditions race organizers would be wise to run a short loop with a well-prepared track, rather than attempt to condition a long stretch of trail. (My Western friends grin when they read about icy tracks. But when you live in the East one of the first things you learn is to deal with situations like this.)

There are many different sleds for use in icy conditions, and most of them operate on the harrow principle. They are heavy and have a bunch of sharp, cutting edges that stick down into the crust and cut it up.

We've even used bulldozers to crush the crust. The bulldozer tracks pulverized the snow all right, but one bulldozer track was just a bit narrow to make a ski track in. In attempting to cut up crusty snow, I've tried rototillers, disc harrows, and weighted planks with spikes.

All of this may sound like lots of work. It is, but if you've had experience putting in tracks with skiers or snowshoers, you know that using a machine and a sled is faster, easier and better.

The timers

You need someone with a cool head here to take over the timing crew. We've had good luck with math teachers in our neck of the woods, or local businessmen who know their numbers.

For timing methods you can go all the way from electric timing to the do-it-yourself method.

Various timing methods

The honor system. You show at the start, log in your starting time and, on completion of the course, log in your finish time. If the course has different start and finish points you will have to synchronize some watches, or start the race and hightail it to the finish before any racers show up. You could start the race by radio or telephone if it was convenient.

An electric timer. Complete with electric eye and a punch-out tape which records the times, this makes the most accurate method of timing. These timers certainly are not necessary for tour races, and actually are just coming into use for our National Championships.

I don't want to get too much into the theory of this, but there is no accuracy advantage in using an electric timer unless you can start the race with it. Therefore, these timers are most convenient when you start the racers at intervals at the same place they are going to finish: under such circumstances timers like these are excellent. All you need is someone to tend the unit and mark down on the tape the numbers of the racers as they start and finish. You then take the tape inside, make your subtractions, and you're all done.

Opting for chronometer plus stop-watches. The most common method of timing these races is by using a mass start and a couple of stop-watches and a chronometer, or master clock. Ideally, you start all the racers simultaneously, using your chronometer and at least one other watch as a back-up. Then when the racers finish, record their times with the chronometer. If you want split-second accuracy, start a stop-watch on the minute, using the chronometer, when you see a racer coming into sight; stop the watch when the racer finishes, and read his time. It might be something like 27.4 seconds on your watch, and you add this to the chronometer time at which you started your stop-watch.

The recorders

I have already mentioned some duties of the timers. According to definition, I suppose, the timers are the fellows who read the watches, tell time, or punch the stop-watches. At our races we usually have one person following the second hand on the chronometer, reading off the seconds: ". . . fifteen, sixteen, seventeen . . ." On the other hand, the recorders are the ones who note the second a racer crosses the finish line and write it on a slip of paper, along with the racer's bib number and the minute he crossed the line.

One timer has the sole job of keeping track of the minute—i.e., the minutes that the race has been in progress.

For instance, the minute-man might have said just a few seconds ago, "This is the one hundred and fiftieth minute." The second man on the chronometer is reading, and a recorder picks up Number 87 as the runner crosses the finish line at the 46th second. The recorder writes down on a slip of paper No. 87–150:46.

This slip of paper is carried to more recorders who, hopefully, are seated at tables in a warm room. If the race has been well organized, these recorders have a card on each racer with the following information (prepared by the secretary while processing entry blanks): name, number, club and starting time. If these cards are in sequential order it's an easy matter to pull out Number 87's card, record his finish time, make the subtraction, have it checked, and then file the card in another pile of finished racers *according to his position as a finisher.*

Mass vs interval starts

Now you can see one advantage to a mass start. The recorders know that everyone started at *zero* minutes, and actually, therefore, the racer's finishing time is his elapsed race time. However, when racers are started at 30-second or one-minute intervals, subtractions are always necessary.

There are other advantages to a mass start:

It's certainly more exciting that the standard interval start.

It's a matter of practicality. If you have a field of 1,000 racers, it would take a long time to get them started, even at 30-second intervals.

Finally, if the watches do fail, the order of finish after a mass start is the order of finish for the race. Not so with an interval start. It's difficult for the spectators and the racers to know the results of an interval start race until the race is actually over and the officials have published the times.

Cross-checks

Order of finish. At all races there should be at least one person who records the order of finish. Sometimes the recorders don't have the time to write down both the racers' bib numbers and the time at which they cross the finish line. If the recorder gets the seconds at which the racers cross he then can check with the person who has the numbers of the order of finish, and match them.

Other timers and officials make mistakes: they're human. They invert numbers, misread bibs, misunderstand times that are read. The order of finish can be invaluable in correcting these and other careless errors. Few races have gone by when we haven't used this information.

Back-up watches. Be sure to have back-up watches. Your chronometer might freeze or stop.

The rules for use of electric timing specify that hand watches must be used as back-ups. This makes good sense. The electric timer might malfunction, as they say. Or there might be a power failure.

Food stations and refreshments

In long, official races of 30 km and over, the organizers are required to provide food stations for the competitors.

"Out of our own test kitchens"

In a tour race you probably won't even need a food station. If you decide to have one, though, or if you want to serve refreshments after the race, here are a few recipes that have proved popular.

Note: A good test for the amount of salt to add is this: If you can just barely taste the salt in the drink, after you mix it ·up, and it tastes a little bit bad to you, it's probably all right for the fellows who will be drinking it after vigorous exercise.

1. Equal parts of tea and cranberry juice. Sugar or dextrose to sweeten and salt to taste.

2. Tea with lemon and sugar or dextrose. Salt if desired.

3. Gatorade or Sportade.

4. Any sweet drink made slightly tart with lemon juice. Salt if desired.

5. Weak coffee with sugar or dextrose.

6. *Finnish Blueberry Drink* prepared as follows: 1 can blueberries, preferably blenderized; 3 cups water; 1 cup sugar; 1 to 2 tablespoons cornstarch. Cook all ingredients except cornstarch to boiling point. Add cornstarch which has been mixed with water. Cook until mixture is thickened. Serve warm.

Note: During a race it's easiest to swallow warm liquids. Don't make them too hot—and don't serve them cold, or else the racers will gag. After the race, the temperatures are the dealer's choice.

You might want to offer two drinks during a race. In that case, it's convenient to label each supply of drink or ask the racer which he prefers.

About lunches. On the entry form the skiers should be given advance notice if there is, or isn't, going to be any food for sale after the race. If you want something more than the quenchers provided by the race committee, you might arrange with a local woman's service club to handle the lunch. Just tell them the number of skiers you expect, give them some ideas—sandwiches, a hearty hot dish, beverages, a sweet— and if they're like the wonderful "ladies aid" groups around our area,

47 Peter Davis of the U.S. Team, tallest internationally known racer, gets refreshment at a food station during a 50-km race.

they'll furnish all the food and be delighted to put the proceeds from the sale into some worthy cause.

Roadways, toilets and parking

To be safe, you should notify all the local authorities about your race. Include the State Police, the sheriff, the selectmen or town officers, the mayor—and Heavens! the big politicians around the areas (if you want to).

Toilet facilities, *at least* at race HQ, are a must. You know how it is.

Years ago I didn't dream that parking would be a problem at x-c races, but that day has arrived. If you have the start and finish at the same place you can be fairly sure everyone who drives in will want to park right there. At one tour race we ran we had only one-lane traffic possible for a stretch of an important road near the Putney School. Had there been a fire or an emergency there could have been serious trouble resulting. Since then we have made efforts to provide ample parking on the school campus.

If you figure one vehicle for every three competitors, even this number can be a sobering thought.

By having the start away from the finish you can split up the parking problem somewhat. This has been a factor in setting courses used for some tour races.

At Sweden's Vasa the organizers have ample parking space, but the competitors have to arrive early enough to make the two-or-three-mile walk to the start. This provides a good warm-up for the 51-mile race which follows!

If your parking is far from the start area and you "have it to do with," as we say, you can provide a shuttle service for the skiers.

First aid

You should have First Aid provisions. At the Washington's Birthday Race in Putney we have been fortunate to have local doctors interested in x-c on hand, and also the Brattleboro Ski Patrol. A good patrol like this can do a great service for any organization.

Someone should be detailed to "sweep the trail" at the end of the race. Occasionally a late skier has got waylaid and needs help.

The press

If you want coverage for your race you should get out some press releases before the event. If the race is big enough you'll have the press there anyway, so you should be prepared.

It's really worth having a special committee to help here. They can make desks, phones and typewriters available; be ready with interesting information on the race and the competitors; drive accredited photographers to vantage points on the course.

If press relations play a good part in your planning, you can send out with the first pre-race publicity story a mimeographed form asking the news media to indicate if they'll be sending a representative to cover the race and if he'll require any special help; if they want total results mailed in; if they want highlights telephoned in (collect) right after the race. Such highlights would include the over-all winner, size of the field, human-interest notes about oldest and youngest finishers and participation by interesting individuals, families or clubs in their news area.

Before the race the secretary, with the help of the press chairman, will have prepared a background fact sheet from material furnished on the entry blanks received before the cut-off date. Also important to have ready is an updated list of assigned numbers and thumbnail identification of the runners. Make plenty of copies of the fact sheet and advance list of numbers, so the news people present can have one of each.

Remember that if you send out advance news releases to spark public interest in your race, you are committed to "repay" the news media by sending them results at the end of the race.

Other special services

Photographs for participants. Sometimes a local professional photographer might want to set up a table in the corner of race HQ to take orders from skiers for a print of themselves in action. However, the race committee should not get involved with this beyond providing space, and of course should have nothing to do with payments or mailing. Often this photographer can make direct arrangements with out-of-town papers to furnish them with race pictures.

Results for participants. Unless getting a corrected set of final results is an automatic award for each finisher, you may want to have skiers bespeak their sets and pay a nominal fee for having them mailed home.

First-class postage on several hundred bulky envelopes can take a good bite out of the race budget. So a system that seems to work is to set up a special table on race day and assign a volunteer to sell large business envelopes to skiers for enough to cover expected postage and handling. Right then and there each skier addresses his envelope to himself, hands it to the volunteer, and it's filed to be stuffed and mailed when the result sheets are ready.

Where it's at

If you're like me, there are days when you want to get out on your own and not follow anyone else's tracks or trails. Then there are other days when you may want to go out with the family, a friend, or a bunch going to a tour race, or perhaps to a sanctioned race for official points in the U.S. rankings.

Therefore I've grouped the different outings in three sections. The first provides a few ideas for going x-c alone or for exploring; the second lists some areas and organizations where you can get information or skiing, or both; and the last is a look at ten of the best-known open tour races in the United States and Canada.

On your own

Because Nordic skiers need far less snow cover than Alpine-resort skiers do, it's almost a truism that you can have a happy x-c junket wherever there's several inches of snow and room to cruise around in.

In the city

If you live in the city or a large town you can always try the municipal recreation areas. In minimal snow cover, investigate the local athletic grounds: many a ski training session has taken place on football and soccer fields.

I've talked with plenty of skiers who have traversed the Cambridge shore of the Charles River (Massachusetts), or buzzed around the Common in Boston and Central Park in New York City. Last year we even had a night race on the lawn in front of the capitol building in Hartford, Connecticut.

48. The Great One   a few of the top-seeded skiers in Sweden's Vasaloppet start for Mora, 85 km and less than five hours away.

In the suburbs

If you live in the suburbs, again you can check with the local recreation department for riding trails, hiking or biking paths, golf courses, race tracks or unplowed back roads. There's always the possibility of some crosslots and farmland touring—but be sure to check with the landowners first.

We once had a relay race outside Stockholm, Sweden, on a horse racetrack. It was a pretty flat course, as you can imagine, but the organizers found a hill behind one of the grandstands and looped the trail up behind it. Aside from this stretch, the spectators could sweep the whole course with their binoculars.

In the country

Then you get into the country and really, with proper permissions, x-c is anywhere there's snow. As I travel around in the wintertime I don't even think, "I wonder if it would be possible to x-c there?" Instead, I imagine how it would be to tour that particular area.

If you're new to a locale but want to do some exploring, ask around town for some hints. Try the postmaster, the town clerk, or the fellows who plow the roads; and don't overlook the proprietors of village gas stations. They'll all have ideas and know skiable terrain.

If you want a definite route you can usually get an old map. Most towns have historic maps of some sort. Or a geodetic survey map will have old roads and trails marked on it.

Naturally, anywhere you see those familiar x-c tracks, you have a lead. Abandoned railroad rights-of-way, certainly on the increase these days, are also good. I've chanced streambeds, frozen over. Try these only when the ice is demonstrably strong enough: be careful, lest you fall through.

Some power-line swaths are easily navigated.

I've always wanted to sneak on to the median of Interstate 91 here in Vermont and take a spin. But the signs say *No Pedestrians,* so I've had to content myself with skiing the sections not yet opened to auto traffic.

Many hiking trails are good. If you have used them during the summer you'll know the terrain.

More organized

There are literally hundreds of places you can go if you're looking for some other skiers or some established touring trails. I can do no more here than list some of the areas I'm most familiar with and make some general suggestions, so the listing is by no means complete. But you can make up your own guide with a bit of research.

First, if you want some fairly good tracks and terrain to ski on, go to a x-c race. You can get out there and see how the racers do it, and after the race, ask permission to try the trail yourself. I strongly recommend this.

If you know a school or college that has a x-c team, chances are good that they will have tracks somewhere most of the winter. Obviously, permission is needed here too.

Nordic clubs and ski touring groups are on the increase, and your local supplier of touring equipment should be able to give you plenty of leads about where good skiable places are.

Don't be afraid to ask Alpine areas what their x-c facilities are like. You'd be surprised at the number of resorts that are developing x-c.

The U.S. Ski Association (1726 Champa Street, Denver, Colorado 80202) can give you addresses of its affiliated ski divisions which are engaged in some sort of official ski touring activity. Ask for the ski-touring committees or councils, or hut committees, in the region you have in mind.

In Canada, write the Canadian Amateur Ski Association (Postal Box 2566, Station D, Ottawa, Ontario) for similar information.

More local areas

One of the most complete booklets of touring information is put out by the Ski Touring Council. Write Rudolf F. Mattesich, Troy, Vermont 05868. Rudi's recommendations are especially good for the eastern United States.

The Viking Ski Club (Box 57, Morin Heights, Province of Quebec, Canada) is a hotbed of activity. The Dominion government has spent $3 million recently on x-c facilities in this province alone.

The North Star Ski Touring Club of Minneapolis, Minnesota, has several organized tours and a very active membership. Write to 4231 Oakdale Avenue South, Minneapolis 55416, or 2409 Fremont Avenue South, Minneapolis 55405.

In Michigan, where ski touring is really picking up, a good bet for information is the Skicrosse Touring Club, 135 Albertson Street, Rochester 48063.

The Nordic Ski Club of Fairbanks, Alaska 99701, is certainly active. In fact, Alaska probably has more x-c activity than any other state in the Union. They have installed x-c in the public school system, Anchorage is a big x-c center, and the U.S. Biathlon Unit trains near by.

The Dartmouth Outing Club (Hanover, New Hampshire 03755) and the Putney Ski Club (Putney, Vermont 05346) usually have something going during the winter. You can almost always find tracks in these two areas.

49. Above, the Gold Rush starts in Colorado. Below (50) is Minnesota's V–J–C Tour, with Alaska's Skiathon below, right (51).

Resort areas

Stratton Mountain in Vermont (zip 05155) was one of the first Alpine areas to offer x-c skiing. They have equipment for sale and some activity.

Vail, in Colorado, has a few professional x-c skiing instructors under Steve Rieschl. They offer lessons, tours in the high country, and they

rent equipment. Write to Rieschl c/o Outdoor Adventures, Box G, Avon, Colorado 81620.

The Trapp Family Lodge in Stowe, Vermont 05672, specializes in touring instruction. Their facilities are complete. Write for their brochure.

Burke Mountain Recreational Area in East Burke, Vermont 05832, has had touring instructors as part of its program for many years.

The Sugarbush Inn, Warren, Vermont 05674, also offers instruction and ski touring.

Another Eastern area is the Acworth Cross-Country Inn in Acworth, New Hampshire 03601. You can write them for reservations and information.

Sven Wiik, transplated Swede and former U.S. Olympic Coach, offers one of the outstanding x-c touring opportunities in the United States at his Scandinavian Lodge at Steamboat Springs, Colorado 80477.

The State of New York has developed a handsome area outside Lake Placid near the famed bobsled run. There is a good network of trails; and completion of the warming hut, including shower facilities, is expected for the 1971—72 season. Write the Lake Placid Chamber of Commerce (zip 12946) for details.

Yosemite National Park has launched a major ski touring program, and information can be had from the Mountaineering School, Yosemite, California 95389.

The Williams Lake resort area in Rosendale, New York 12472, has fine x-c ski facilities.

The city of Glens Falls, New York 12801, has one of the few lighted trails in the United States for night x-c skiing.

Some utilities companies are beginning to develop their land for x-c recreation. The Northeast Utilities Service Company in Northfield, Massachusetts 01360, is one example.

Summarizing: There are countless sources for impromptu or semi-organized x-c outings. The ideas listed above merely give you something to start from. Remember that state development/recreation departments can help you with information already prepared; an inquiry addressed to the department, in the capital, will be forwarded to the person best able to answer you. Don't forget the winter-sports editor of the local newspaper in the bailiwick where you want to ski (it's a courtesy here to include a stamped, self-addressed envelope).

And you can always get together with friends to start your own group. I'm not kidding.

Tour races

Here are ten annual, established tour races, with bits of information about each. In general, the races are open to all competitors regardless of ability, age or sex, but if you're interested in joining the fun you should write to the organizers ahead of time and get the most accurate details you can.

Time will tell if these races represent the beginning of a continuing series of events open to tourskiers on this continent. In Sweden, the Vasaloppet will be coming up to its fiftieth running in 1973, and at the rate *they're* going they will have over 10,000 for that one.

With many tourskiers it becomes a matter of pride to complete the local tour race each year. You may get hooked yourself. In Sweden they say you're not a man until you've finished the Vasa. Well, in 1968, one-thousandth of that country's population finished the 85-km classic. In the United States the equivalent field would be 200,000!

The Washington's Birthday Tour (Vermont)

The first Washington's Birthday Ski Touring Race was conceived by Eric Barradale of Guilford, Vermont, back in 1963. Right now, this event probably ranks as the oldest and largest regularly run tour race in the United States.

Forty competitors ran the first year, and since then the numbers have increased to a record 600 in 1970, drawn from all over the Northeastern United States and nearby parts of Canada. The Putney School has assumed management of the race for the time being, but the 1972 version will be run by a group in Dr. Barradale's home town of Guilford.

The course has varied from 10 to 20 km, and anyone is eligible to enter the tour. For information write the Race Committee, Putney School, Putney, Vermont 05346.

Madonna Vasa (Vermont)

The first Madonna Vasa was held in 1965, and utilizes the same 24-km course every year. The race is held on the first Sunday in March to coincide with *the* Vasa in Sweden. Racers start at the ski area parking lot at Madonna Mountain at 30-second intervals, and finish on the Mountain Road in Underhill Center. It goes across some rugged terrain and, while everyone who wants to can enter, rank beginners should check out the course first.

For information write Dr. John Bland, Upper Valley Road, Cambridge, Vermont 05444.

Stowe Derby (Vermont)

The Derby has been going since 1965. In 1971 there were 15 classes and 75 runners. The course starts at Handy's West Hill in Stowe, and the competitors can elect to run either 2½ or nearly 7 miles. For information write Jack Handy, Stowe School, Stowe, Vermont 05672.

Canadian Marathon (near Montreal)

This just may be the longest race in the world, run on 80 of the 100 miles of the Montreal-to-Ottawa trail. The event, which takes two days (you might have guessed this!), was first run in 1967 as part of Canada's Centennial, and in 1971 there were 600 participants.

The Marathon is open to racing or touring single runners, two-man teams, four-man teams, and juniors. The teams can run as a relay, and juniors who complete 20, 30 or 40 miles get medals. Teams also may be made up of any mixture of ages and sexes.

There are food stations every 10 miles, the course is checked and swept. Anyone is eligible. The date for it is usually the end of February.

Write Jan Nordstrom, Viking Ski Club, P.O. Box 57, Morin Heights, Province of Quebec, for information.

V–J–C Ski Tour (Minnesota)

First held in 1971, this trek in Viking country was an immediate success, with nearly 300 skiers completing the tour. The course—southwest of Minneapolis—starts in Victoria, goes through Jonathan, and ends in Chaska: hence hence the name "VJC."

The event is run in late February and is open to all. For information write to North Star Ski Touring Club, 4231 Oakdale Avenue, Minneapolis, Minnesota 55416.

The Gold Rush (Colorado)

The Gold Rush was instituted in 1971, and at the first running there were more than 300 finishers. The course starts near Breckenridge, Colorado, over 10,000 feet up on the Continental Divide, and finishes 10 km later at the Summit County High School in Frisco. The emphasis is on family skiers—or "citizen skiers," as they're called in the West. Write the Frisco Chamber of Commerce (zip 80433).

John Craig Memorial (Oregon)

This race was run off and on a few times during the 1930's, '40's and '50's, but was not permanently established until 1970, when the Oregon Nordic Club took over.

The event is named after John Craig, an Oregon pioneer who helped to build, by hand, the first road across rugged McKenzie Pass, over a mile high in the Cascade Range. Later, Craig carried mail across the pass during winter, and now, in his honor, each skier carries mail during the race. (The mail is hand-canceled at the finish with a commemorative postmark, then forwarded to the local Blue River post office for normal delivery.)

The course goes over the pass, east to west, from snowline to snowline, and averages about 18 miles in length. The race is usually held the first weekend in April unless there is a conflict with Easter.

For information write Ed Park, Bend Chapter, Oregon Nordic Club, Bend, Oregon 97701; or Jay Bowerman, McKenzie View Drive, Eugene, Oregon 97401.

Yosemite (California)

Another fun race was initiated during the 1970–71 winter in Yosemite National Park. A 10-km course was laid out, and around 70 skiers participated. The day after the tour a few team-relays were held, and this competition is planned for future years as an added attraction. Write Yosemite Mountaineering School in California (zip 95389) for details.

Fairbanks Skiathon (Alaska)

The Lathrop High School Ski Team originated the Skiathon in 1965, and now the Nordic Ski Club of Fairbanks has assumed responsibility for the event. The course uses the Sharland Ski Trails and is about 20 km long. The race is held around March 20th, to coincide with the vernal equinox. The field has averaged between 200 and 300 runners. For further information write the Nordic Ski Club of Fairbanks, Fairbanks, Alaska 99701.

Glacier Stampede (Alaska)

The Nordic Ski Club of Fairbanks (address immediately above) and the Alaska Alpine Club combine to run this unusual tour. The course starts about halfway between Fairbanks and Anchorage on the Richardson Highway, and climbs 8 miles up Cantwell Glacier to an Alpine cabin. Here's the twist: each skiers must pack a tent, sleeping bag and provisions for the overnight stay. The Stampede is generally held the end of April, and in 1971 some 220 skiers participated. Write the Fairbanks club for information.

52. He's five years old and he finished the race. And just maybe he is what it's all about, when you get right down to it.